OXFORD

INTRODUCTION & GUIDE
CHRIS ANDREWS & DAVID HUELIN

© Chris Andrews Publications, Oxford. Tel 01865 723404
All rights reserved. First published 1990 Revised edition 1999

Photographs by Chris Andrews & Angus Palmer
Text by David Huelin
Design G & C Andrews

Produced and Published by Chris Andrews Publications
1 North Hinksey Village Oxford OX2 ONA Tel 01865 723404
Printed and bound in Great Britain by
Butler & Tanner Ltd, Frome and London

INTRODUCTION

Oxford is one of England's most pictured and most written-about cities; this present addition to the crowd of existing books is nevertheless offered as a fresh view of the place, to serve both as an introduction and as a lasting reminder. The text begins with a historical sketch of city and university and continues with a simple guide to the principal buildings – without apology, but with grateful acknowledgement, to the publications from which facts have been filched and opinions purloined. The photographs attempt to portray the best of this elusively handsome city.

PRINCIPAL CONTENTS

Introduction to Oxford

OXFORD may be seen as a seat of intellectual activity advancing the frontiers of knowledge, fostering the achievements of Roger Bacon, John Wycliffe, Robert Boyle, Edmund Halley, Howard Florey, and many others. Also it is the birthplace of the *Oxford English Dictionary*, the ultimate authority on the language, now in its up-to-date twenty-volume second edition.

OXFORD is the background of *Alice* and her wonderful world, of Thomas Hardy's *Jude the Obscure*, of Matthew Arnold's *Thyrsis*, of Dorothy Sayers' *Gaudy Night*, and of countless poems, novels, and fantasies. Shelley, sent down for professing atheism, Gerard Manley Hopkins, curate of St Aloysius R.C.Church; Michael Innes, a don behind a pseudonym; T.E. Lawrence, C.S. Lewis, J. R. R. Tolkein, Evelyn Waugh, John Betjeman, Nevill Coghill – they all owe something to Oxford, as do many others in less evident ways.

OXFORD gave a home to the Stuart Court – that 'centre of corruption and good taste' – when King Charles had his capital here from 1642 to 1646. At all times in history Oxford has nurtured statesmen, countless bishops and not a few archbishops, as well as pioneers, colonizers, and political leaders – including William Penn, James Oglethorpe, Cecil Rhodes, and more than twenty British Prime Ministers in the past two centuries. Oxford has seen the birth of religious movements inspired by men such as the Wesley brothers, and John Keble.

OXFORD may be seen materially as a concentration of handsome buildings dating from as early as AD 1000, with an especially good representation of the 15th to the 18th centuries; here are fine examples of the work of William Orchard, Christopher Wren, Nicholas Hawksmoor, James Gibbs, and the Oxford amateurs Dean Henry Aldrich and Dr George Clarke. The great Victorian architects are prominent too; the Gilbert Scott family, William Butterfield, Basil Champneys, and Thomas G. Jackson.

OXFORD: the name may for some people conjure up tutorials and lectures attended when ostensibly, or earnestly, reading for a degree; or the tranquillity of riverside walks in the University Parks or Christ Church Meadow, and Commemoration Balls on warm summer nights. For boating enthusiasts Oxford can mean the finest reaches of the upper Thames or the most idyllic stretch of the lower Cherwell with a leisurely punt on a sunny day. Then there is Eights Week – dramatized for posterity in Max Beerbohm's *Zuleika Dobson*.

OXFORD has been lived in and loved or hated, but never ignored or forgotten, by a thousand years of Kings, Queens, philosophers, prelates, scientists, students, dons, and plain people.

Opposite: Radcliffe Square

The Place. The Romans left nothing permanent in this part of the Thames valley and came no nearer to Oxford than Headington; but by the year AD 700 a settlement had grown up round the crossing of two major trade routes; one between London and the West, along the Thames valley to the Severn, and the other linking the south coast ports with the Midlands. The routes probably crossed near the point now known as Carfax (Carrefour) and both must have used fords over the Rivers Thames and Cherwell.

The hamlet came to be called Oxnaforda; it acquired importance by being on the border of the rival kingdoms of Mercia and Wessex and becoming a meeting place for Kings and their barons, as well as being a fortified post on the Thames against marauding Danes. When the two kingdoms were united Oxnaforda was in a commanding central position and in the 11th century became almost an alternative to Winchester as capital of the kingdom. After the Norman Conquest the town was further fortified and garrisoned; beginning about 1070, the Norman governor Robert d'Oilly built the massive walls with six towers, of which one remains, and the Mound, originally surmounted by a timber look-out post. He also set up a chapel and living quarters for a few monks. This small community of St George-in-the-Castle never became large or important but it made a contribution to Oxford's emergence as a seat of study, if only by sheltering Geoffrey of Monmouth, who in 1139 completed a readable version of the Arthurian legends in his *Historia Britonum*.

Matilda and Stephen. The only action involving the Castle was during the civil war between King Stephen, who had seized the English throne and his cousin Matilda, who had a better claim to it. Just before her coronation, when she had virtually won the contest, she antagonized

Winter Dawn, Port Meadow

the people of London and provoked so violent an uprising that she was forced to flee, and she took refuge in Oxford Castle. Stephen, from the comforts of Beaumont Palace, built by Henry I, laid siege to the Castle for some three months in the hard winter of 1141–2. Matilda and a few companions were lowered on ropes from the castle wall by night and, all dressed in white, escaped across the frozen Thames and through the snow to Abingdon, or possibly Wallingford.

Christ Church Cathedral

Origins of the University. The earliest antecedents of learning in Oxford may be traced, rather tenuously, back to about AD 720 when the local ruler King Didan founded for his devout daughter Frideswide a nunnery, built where Christ Church Cathedral now stands.[1]

After Frideswide's death the nunnery eventually came to an end, and the buildings were occupied from about 1120 by a community of Augustinian monks. They restored the decaying structures, and in 1150–75 rebuilt the little chapel as a large priory church dedicated to St Frideswide which, somewhat modified, survives as today's Cathedral. The priory school was probably the first place of learning set up in Oxford, except perhaps for the community of St-George-in-the-Castle. Oxford's status was also enhanced by the founding in 1129 of Oseney Priory (later Abbey), where another priory school was established. Oxford gained importance under King Henry I (reigned 1100–35) who, having built Beaumont Palace just outside the walls of the Castle, spent much of his time here. The presence of the King and his Court was itself an attraction for ambitious scholars. Moreover King Henry 'Beauclerk', as his sobriquet implies, was himself a scholar and did much to encourage learning at Oxford. At this time all students had received the tonsure and were in secular holy orders; they were of humble origins and, beginning as boys in the monastery schools, were following the only course open to intelligent but poor young men seeking to better themselves: that was scholarship within the Church, where remunerative parish livings and comfortable chaplaincies with the nobility were the main prizes. With the King and Court at Beaumont Palace there was nowhere better than Oxford for obtaining preferment.

Oseney Abbey. Robert d'Oilly the younger, nephew and successor to the builder of the Castle, in 1129 founded for the Augustinians a priory on the island of Oseney in the Thames outside the city walls. The priory became an abbey and the school contributed to the fame that Oxford was beginning to acquire as a centre of learning.

In the equally long reign of Henry II,[2] who also lived at Beaumont Palace, Oxford's renown as a seat of learning continued to spread, especially after 1167 when, during Henry's quarrel with the French, the English scholars at the University of Paris were obliged to come home.

Many came to Oxford bringing experience of the teaching system in force since about AD 800 at Paris, already a well-established *studium generale* or place of general study; in fact the foremost university of Europe.

Before the year 1200 Oxford had been recognized as a *studium generale*; the teachers had begun to call themselves 'Masters' and they formed a secular religious guild known as *universitas* (meaning the whole body of Masters and Doctors). Learning was the exclusive domain of the Church, and by the end of the 12th century the guild had been duly recognized by the Bishop of Lincoln, who in 1214 appointed a Chancellor to regulate it.

Chancellor Grosseteste. The Bishop of Lincoln, whose Diocese included Oxford, appointed a Chancellor as his episcopal delegate; (later the Masters won the right to elect their own Chancellor). One of the Bishop's earliest appointments around 1224 was Robert Grosseteste (1168–1253), a scholar and a Master of Oxford, who was a man of outstanding erudition and himself became Bishop of Lincoln in 1234. During his ten years as Chancellor of the guild, Grosseteste greatly advanced Oxford's status in the 13th-century revival of learning in Europe, and he strongly supported the scholastic activities of the Mendicant Friars when they arrived in Oxford.

The Proctors. The office of the Proctors is first mentioned in 1248, and in practice may have existed earlier. In the 13th century the scholars had divided themselves into two 'nations', North and South, and each nation chose its own regent or Proctor. The Proctors were not particularly concerned with the rivalries of the two nations, but each was responsible to the Regent

Encaenia

Masters for his group's discipline. When the nations forgot their differences towards the end of the 13th century the Proctors' roles were merged but not substantially altered. With the addition in 1961 of the post of Assessor there are in effect three Proctors.

The Proctors have traditionally been Fellows of colleges in a rota of pairs; they retain wide powers and have inherited administrative, and even liturgical, duties including extensive 'watch-dog' functions. They are best known for their disciplinary role among the undergraduates, somewhere between policemen and nannies. Some years ago, when the late Professor Nevill Coghill was a young Fellow of Exeter College, with his sympathies on the side of the undergraduates, the conjunction of his proctorial duties and the long Proctor's gown prompted him to say that he felt like a combination of Charley's Aunt and Judas Iscariot.

Town and Gown. The Domesday survey of 1086 showed that the population of Oxford had declined from some four thousand in Saxon times – it was a major English town as recorded in the Anglo-Saxon Chronicle of 912 – to little more than one thousand after the Conquest, when there were many empty houses. The influx of scholars in the following century, especially after the migration from Paris in 1167, led to a disproportion between citizens and scholars reflected in a continual antagonism of 'Town' and 'Gown', punctuated by fights and riots during the two centuries following. The town reluctantly accepted the academic population as customers for its goods and services and profited accordingly, but the University was in no such dependence on the town; until the 1420s the Masters owned no building of importance and had no roots to hold them. They were free to move to other towns, which they did more than once in the 13th and 14th centuries when riots in Oxford threatened Masters' and students' lives.[3]

Monks and Friars. The Augustinian monks of St Frideswide's Priory and of Oseney Abbey, the Cistercians at Rewley Abbey from 1280, and the small monastic community of St George-in-the-Castle, all contributed to the tradition of study at Oxford. Monks, however, were contemplative scholars who sought no influence in the secular world; it was to the zealous, adventurous, intellectually brilliant Mendicant Friars, who came in the 13th century, that Oxford owed much of the fame that it acquired throughout Europe. The principal Orders of Mendicant Friars in Oxford – though not the only ones – were the Dominicans (Blackfriars), who came in 1221 and established here the first Dominican house in England, and the Franciscans (Greyfriars), who came in 1224 and chose Robert Grosseteste to be their Rector. Both these Orders set up large communities, each with a membership of 80 to 90 by the end of the century. Besides their numbers, the friars were of formidable scholastic ability.

The leading intellects among the Dominicans in the 13th century were Albertus Magnus the 'Universal Doctor' and his pupil Thomas Aquinas the 'Angelic Doctor'. The Oxford house did not include any member of such world-famous calibre, but it had many able men to disseminate Thomist teaching. The Franciscans, on the other hand, encouraged by their brilliant Rector, concentrated in Oxford some of their best scholars: Adam Marsh the 'Illustrious Doctor', John Duns Scotus the 'Subtle Doctor' – whose followers were later labelled *dunces* by their opponents – William Ockham the 'Invincible Doctor', and the most famous of all Grosseteste's pupils, Roger Bacon, the 'Marvellous Doctor', who had such a wide-ranging inquisitive mind, and conducted such strange experiments, that his Superiors accused him of practising necromancy, and imprisoned him for ten years, depriving him of writing materials.

Academic Halls. By the beginning of the 13th century the foundations of the teaching system and the syllabus had been laid down, but there was little formal practice; Masters were lecturing to disorderly gatherings of students wherever a room could be hired. For discipline, as well as for protection from a hostile town, the Masters began to gather students into halls of residence, where some kind of order could be enforced, even though no teaching were done. By the end of the century it had been decreed that students had to be enrolled ('matriculated') at a recognized academic hall under an authorized Regent Master; and so teaching began in the halls. The names of some two hundred halls have been recorded, and it is believed that as many as eighty – some no doubt quite small – may have existed at any one time in the 13th and 14th centuries. The medieval academic halls were a natural development of the simple hostels or lodging houses where scholars lived; they were precursors of the colleges in that they offered protection, board, bed, and later some tuition, to enrolled or matriculated scholars, but they were impermanent. The continuance of an academic hall depended on the competence of its Principal or Master, who had annually to obtain his licence from the University.

The colleges, however, were able to do more effectively everything that the halls did; they had their endowments and their income, they owned the buildings, they had permanent status and autonomous government by elected Fellows; they were answerable only to their respective Visitors, not to the University. It was a logical development that, as the colleges increased in number, size, and wealth, the halls declined and were absorbed by the vastly richer colleges.

Halls reappeared in the 19th century as Private Halls offering matriculation and undergraduate status to students, and accommodation at a more modest cost than the college norm. These halls too were impermanent, however, since each was authorized by the University in the name of the Principal whose personal business venture it was, and it would cease or change its name if he were to give it up. Some Private Halls, nevertheless, became quite eminent. Since 1918 a new designation of Permanent Private Hall allows a hall to be owned by a corporate body and to be affiliated to the University so that its students may graduate. Such a hall may acquire full collegiate status, as for example St Peter's and the women's colleges did.

First Colleges. The second half of the 13th century saw the founding of the first three colleges: University College, Balliol and Merton. These foundations were secular responses to the monasteries and were intended to benefit scholars until then living in hired buildings insecurely and at a material disadvantage by comparison with the 'regulars' – monks and friars in their well-regulated and well-protected communities. The colleges, unlike the academic halls, had proper endowments and owned their buildings; even so, at first they gave shelter only to Doctors, Masters, and selected scholars.

The question of which of the first three colleges is the oldest rests on the definition of 'foundation': the endowment or bequest, the ownership of buildings, or the approval of statutes. University College ('Univ') was founded with a legacy that William, Archdeacon of Durham, who died in 1249, left to the University to set up a community of ten Masters in a suitable house; this society did not receive its statutes until thirty years later in 1280, and did

Balliol

Merton

University

not occupy buildings of its own until 1331, eighty years after the bequest. Meanwhile John de Balliol, at the command of the Bishop of Durham, about 1263 bought or built a house for sixteen poor scholars; he died and his widow Princess Dervorguilla completed the endowment, but she did not provide statutes until 1284, four years after Univ. Walter de Merton set up his college of twenty scholars in 1264; he had completed some of his buildings by 1266, a little later than Balliol, but his endowment was made at the same time, and his definitive statutes were approved by 1274, earlier than those of the other two colleges.

William of Wykeham (1323–1404). The most important of the foundations of the 14th century was New College, 1379, planned, endowed, and supervised by the greatest innovator of his age: William of Wykeham, Bishop of Winchester. He was a man of humble birth and of great ability; he was Clerk of the King's Works at Windsor Castle, where he gained experience of building practice. In 1367 he became Bishop of Winchester and Chancellor of the Realm; thus at the age of forty-four he held the richest ecclesiastical office and the best-paid secular position in the kingdom.

The statutes of New College required that all the subjects in the university curriculum should be taught within the college and that the scholars should live under one roof with their tutors, the resident Masters; these two requirements combined to give to college life a new significance, which in time reached the other colleges and resulted in the gradual disappearance of the less progressive unendowed old halls. The innovation of including the scholars as residents of a defensible, disciplined, house contributed to the increased stability of the University in times of social unrest.

William of Wykeham also founded a school in Winchester to prepare boys for a university education, and New College to give them that education. His innovations, designed to make the college self-contained and independent, had the effect of creating a university within the University, and in fact New College obtained the right to examine its own scholars for

New College Cloister

degrees and to vouch for them before the University without further examination. This right was maintained into the 19th century.

William of Wykeham made another contribution to college life when he built New College as a closed quadrangle with chapel, dining hall, library, lecture rooms, and living quarters on its four sides, the rooms being arranged on separate staircases, as if in a terrace of houses. The quadrangle arrangement, closed up with stout gates, was defensible against a hostile town, as had been demonstrated when college buildings sheltered many scholars during the St Scholastica riots of 1354.

John Wycliffe. While New College was being built another notable man was making his mark on Oxford. John Wycliffe (1320–1384) was probably a Fellow of Merton, perhaps Warden of *Canterbury College*, a resident at one time of Queen's, and briefly Master of Balliol. Although he is perhaps best known now for his English translation of the Bible – a work of profound scholarship to which he devoted a great part of his life – it was as a critic of superstition and corruption that he was most noted in his own time. His denunciations of the many abuses in the Church brought him a large following, ranging from intellectuals who supported his radical religious ideas, to simpler people who resented seeing a rich Church and fat friars growing richer and fatter at the expense of many starving peasants. Wycliffe was a protestant two centuries before the Reformation. He and his followers, the Lollards, were persecuted by the Church and in 1377 he was arraigned of heresy and was expelled from Oxford. He retired to his rectory at Lutterworth, leaving a legacy of enlightened thinking that made the University receptive to the new ideas of the Renaissance and the Reformation.

All the copies of Wycliffe's writings that could be found were of course burned; however, a group of Bohemian scholars succeeded in returning to Prague with many of his original manuscripts, which were welcomed by the reformer John Huss (1369–1415).

University and Colleges. By the end of the 14th century, after the founding of New College in 1379, there were seven endowed colleges with Heads, Resident Masters (later called Fellows), scholars (aspiring to become Masters), and an increasing number of resident fee-paying students; these foundations owned substantial buildings and, together with the still numerous halls of residence and the monastic colleges, accounted for the university population. The growth of the number and wealth of the colleges was in contrast with the slow material development of the University.

The Masters had established the curriculum, the system of teaching, examinations by disputation, and the conferring of degrees; but the academic structure had no proper physical setting; St Mary's Church was used for disputations, lectures, judicial proceedings and ceremonies of all kinds. The University owned no building until 1320 when the original Congregation House was built adjoining the church; it was little more than a debating chamber, with the beginnings of a library above, and was hardly worthy of the *studium generale*.

The University in the Fifteenth Century. The *universitas* began to acquire a more tangible presence. In 1426 the first university-owned 'schools' or lecture rooms were built to replace the ancient houses in Schools Street – along the west side of what is now Radcliffe Square – which until then had served for teaching but had become inadequate. The buildings put up by the University from 1426 onwards were on the site of today's Old Schools Quadrangle now occupied by the Bodleian Library. Of the 15th-century buildings only the Divinity School, with Duke Humfrey's Library above it, remains in its original form. Humfrey Duke of Gloucester (1391–1447), younger brother of Henry V, began giving to the University his great collection of books and manuscripts, and money to build a library to house them.

Duke Humfrey's Library

Duke Humfrey's Library, eventually set up in the 1480s was perhaps the crowning achievement of the University in the 15th century. The buildings were in effect the first identifiable seat of the Masters' activities. Deplorably, Duke Humfrey's Library was destroyed by the vandals of the extremist Puritan Visitation of 1549, though the building survived.

Three more colleges were founded in this 15th century, bringing to ten the number of fully endowed houses with permanent buildings and communities of Masters, scholars, and students. The principle, established by William of Wykeham in the previous century at New College, of students' residing and being taught in college (reading with a Master) had become general and was developing into what is now known as the tutorial system.

Monastic Colleges. The Benedictines began sending scholars to Oxford as early as 1175, and a century later established two houses of their own: *Durham College* (1286) for scholars from their abbeys in the north of England, and *Gloucester College* (1283) for the abbeys in the south. In the same period, 1280, Edmund, Earl of Cornwall, founded for the Cistercians a *studium* in Oxford; it grew from being merely a college and became *Rewley Abbey*. In 1363 Archbishop Islip founded *Canterbury College* for the monks of Christ Church, Canterbury; it began as a college for regulars (monks) but later admitted seculars as well. It was notable for having John Wycliffe as Warden for a short time before it reverted to wholly regular membership. In the following century Archbishop Chichele (founder of All Souls) set up *St Bernard's College* in

Oxford from the north

1437 for the Cistercians; in 1435 the Augustinians had founded *St Mary's Hall* where Erasmus stayed in 1498–1500. The great Abbeys of Oseney and Rewley were dissolved in 1539, and their buildings in time disappeared. The five monastic colleges were closed, and all the Mendicant Friars departed, leaving only a few street names in Oxford.

The Humanists. In the middle years of the 14th century Wycliffe's penetrating mind had revealed to eager Oxford audiences the futility of the narrow arguments that preoccupied medieval scholasticism. Towards the end of the following century, and into the early years of the 16th, an intellectual advance of comparable importance was made by the Humanists – those who studied and taught the classical humanities, especially as contained in ancient Greek language and literature: 'the great or classical achievements of humanity in literature and art'. They brought the Renaissance to Oxford and dispelled the last remnants of scholasticism, which survived among a

Corpus Christi

few reactionary 'Trojans' opposing the Greek advance. When Erasmus was in Oxford he was greatly impressed by the Humanists – Grocyn, Colet, Linacre, and Thomas More – and wrote enthusiastically about them.

When Bishop Richard Fox founded Corpus Christi College in 1517 he not only made provision for a lectureship in Greek, the first in Oxford, but he also established a trilingual library of Humanist works in Latin, Greek, and Hebrew, which was much admired by Erasmus who predicted that more scholars would come to Corpus than would go to Rome.

Despite Wycliffe's enlightened preaching in the 14th century, the Humanists in the late 15th still found among the 'Trojans' resistance to the teaching of classical Greek philosophy and literature. There were still a few Nominalists and Realists and other reactionaries who were concerned with questions such as whether Learning can save the Soul; whether Predestination foredooms everyone to Salvation or Damnation; how it is that all Nature obeys Reason, except Mankind. The Trojans were so obstructive that they were admonished by Henry VIII and by Cardinal Wolsey; the displeasure of such eminent persons apparently weakened the resistance.

The Reformation and the Dissolution. King Henry VIII may have used the Reformation of the Church and the Dissolution of the Monasteries for his own ends, but fortunately for Oxford he respected learning and saw the need to have secular friends; he firmly put down the 'greedy wretches' who would have dissolved the colleges for the sake of their revenues.

'Whereas we had a regard only to pull down sin by defacing the monasteries,
you have a desire also to overthrow all goodness, by subversion of Colleges.
I tell you, sir, that I judge no land in England better bestowed than that which
is given to our Universities, for by their maintenance. Our realm shall be self-
governed when we be dead and rotten. I love not learning so ill that I will impair
the revenues of any one house by a penny whereby it may be upholden.'

The disruptions caused by Henry VIII were unsettling for the University; nevertheless Henry at this time gave his support to Cardinal Wolsey's ambitious plans for a grand college to surpass all others – known first as Cardinal College and later as Christ Church.

Visitations. After the Reformation the Universities were no longer governed by the ultimate authority of the Pope, but by the English Crown. They were virtually the only sources of parish priests, and the Sunday sermon was then the principal means of shaping public opinion; the Crown therefore had to ensure that the teaching at the Universities was politically as well as theologically correct – a process well described as 'tuning the pulpit'.

The changing political and religious intentions of successive governments reached Oxford in the form of royal commissions known as Visitations; there were five Visitations in the 16th century, and the scholars and Masters were 'much troubled and hurried up and down by the changes in religion'. The Visitors were given wide powers; they could purge the colleges of recalcitrant Heads and Fellows; they could modify the statutes and the internal affairs of the colleges; they could change the University syllabus and impose specific teaching obligations or prohibitions; they were feared and hated by the dons.

The reforms and upheavals imposed by Henry VIII were followed in the brief reign of Edward VI by further ruthless advances in Protestantism, and by bigotry and vandalism perpetrated by the Puritan Visitation of 1549, who destroyed Duke Humfrey's Library.

'Bloody' Mary and the Protestant Martyrs. Then followed the accession in 1553 of the adamantly Roman Catholic Queen Mary Tudor, who in a reign of only five years succeeded in having some two hundred and seventy Protestant churchmen in England burned for heresy. The most prominent among her victims were the three Bishops burned at the stake in Oxford in 1555 and 1556, commemorated by the Martyrs' Memorial in St Giles. Thomas Cranmer, Archbishop of Canterbury; Hugh Latimer, Bishop of Worcester; and Nicholas Ridley, Bishop of Rochester, all Cambridge graduates and staunch Protestants, were arraigned of heresy in

1554 and brought to Oxford to face a disputation with a group of Roman Catholic divines in St Mary's Church. The three bishops were then held for some eighteen months in the Bocardo Prison, which adjoined the Church of St Michael-at-the-North-Gate. In the autumn of 1555 Latimer and Ridley were formally tried and condemned at St Mary's, and were burned at the stake 'in the Towne Ditch, over against Balliol College'. Cranmer had been made Archbishop by the Pope, and the case against him had to be referred to the Vatican, which meant a longer delay. Finally in 1556 he was tried and condemned at St Mary's, degraded at Christ Church Cathedral, and burned at the same spot, outside Balliol.

Elizabeth I. In the reign of Elizabeth I (1558–1603) some thirty Oxford priests – Fellows of colleges – were put to death for practising Catholic rites or refusing to recognise the Queen as spiritual head of the Church; such recalcitrance was seen as sedition or treason and punished accordingly. Among the martyrs the best known is Edmund Campion, of St John's College, who was executed at Tyburn in 1581.

Elizabeth saw the Church of England firmly established; she needed to be sure that what was taught at the universities was politically as well as theologically acceptable, and that there were no traitors or subversives at work. At Oxford her 'favourite', Robert Dudley, Earl of Leicester, was Chancellor in 1564–88; in his university charter of 1571 he skilfully introduced a degree of indirect state supervision.

Queen Elizabeth enjoyed visiting Oxford; she came in 1566 and again in 1592; she listened to orations and disputations, and she held her own in academic debate, in Latin. On both

Oxford and flooded Christ Church Meadow

occasions her leave-taking was gracious. At the end of her first visit in 1566, after several days of academic exercises, she took her leave with an elegant speech.

'Since I came to Oxford I have seen and heard many things; I have been delighted with them all. For myself I have had many teachers, who tried to make me learned, but they worked upon barren soil. I know I am not worthy of your praises. But if my speech be full of barbarisms I will end it with a prayer: that you may prosper greatly in my lifetime and be happy for generations after I am dead'.

At the end of her second visit in 1592, Elizabeth's often-quoted valediction was:

'Farewell, farewell, dear Oxford; God bless thee and increase thy sons in number, holiness and virtue"

The Earl of Leicester made an important innovation by transferring the government of the University from the unwieldy assembly of Regent Masters (the Lesser Congregation) to a new more manageable group made up of the Heads of Houses; he used this new group as a kind of caucus round the Chancellor (himself) with the role of making recommendations to the Great Congregation (now Convocation). This group of Heads was confirmed and enlarged in later statutes and is today the Hebdomadal Council. Convocation is the larger assembly of Masters, Regent or not, resident or not, which meets seldom but is the ultimate authority within Oxford's system of self-government; Congregation is the smaller body of resident Regent Masters.

Bodleian Library. In Elizabeth's reign Oxford received one of its most important benefactions. Sir Thomas Bodley (1545–1613) a Fellow of Merton College, retired from the Queen's diplomatic service in 1598 and set about reconstructing Duke Humfrey's library, destroyed by the Puritan Visitation of 1549. Bodley restored Duke Humfrey's 15th-century building, empty since the Visitation; he was then so successful in obtaining gifts and purchases of books, besides his own, that the original building soon proved too small. In 1612 Bodley added the east wing, known as the Arts End, with its ground floor as the *proscholium* or ante-chamber to the Divinity School hall, filling one side of the quadrangle. He left a legacy for the building of what is now the Old Schools Quadrangle, stipulating that the upper storey be reserved for the ever-growing library, leaving the two lower floors as schools or lecture halls. The buildings were put up between 1613 and 1619; tradition has it that work began on the day of Bodley's funeral. Today the Library occupies all the buildings that form the quadrangle, and the Schools are in the High Street. This was not only the foundation of one of the world's greatest libraries but also a notable addition to the architectural aspect of the University.

About 1636 William Laud, when he was Chancellor of the University, put a finishing touch to Bodley's great work by adding a west wing to match the eastern Arts End; the wing is known as the Selden End from the valuable collection of Persian, Turkish and Chinese books given by John Selden (1584–1654), an erudite academic and one of the first MPs for the University. The ground floor contains the Convocation House and the Court-room.

The so-called *New Bodleian* is an extension of the main library, with which it is connected by underground passages. It is part of the now fully computerized Bodleian system embracing a hundred academic and specialized libraries in Oxford that collectively give access to some six million books and over one million maps.

The Selden End, Bodleian Library

Scholars after the Reformation. The colleges founded before the Reformation were governed by statutes obliging them to maintain 'indigent scholars' – that is, clever boys of humble origin – whose only means of advancement was by scholarship within the Church. The system produced brilliant churchmen-statesmen who, in the age of a barely literate nobility, stand out as the intellectual leaders; Robert Grosseteste, William of Wykeham, William Wayneflete, Thomas Wolsey, William Laud, were all of humble origin.

The Reformation changed the character of the University by eliminating the dominance of the Church, cutting off the supply of monastic scholars, and making a university education available and attractive to laymen from the increasingly literate nobility and the emerging

19

middle classes; these young men came to Oxford not as indigent scholars in holy orders but as fee-paying laymen or 'gentlemen commoners' which made them welcome guests; but they tended to crowd out the poor scholars.

The endowed grammar schools founded in the 17th century did not fully replace the dissolved monasteries as nurseries of scholars; for the many boys not fortunate enough to reach the University by means of a school bursary or a college scholarship, the only other way was to be admitted to a college as *a servitor* – a status invented for the benefit of the gentlemen commoners. The servitors' lot was to perform menial and other tasks for the gentlemen (including writing essays or dissertations) in exchange for which they were given the poorest of living quarters and such tuition as they could come by.

The undergraduate social strata in the 17th and 18th centuries were: Nobleman, Gentleman Commoner, Commoner, Servitor. The designation *undergraduate*, applying to all of these, came into use about 1630. The colleges continued to elect Scholars, but these were full members of their colleges, whereas the others were more like paying guests.

James I. King James was proud of his erudition; he enjoyed coming to Oxford and exchanging learned witticisms with the dons. In the benign climate of the early 17th century there was a great increase in academic activity and a broadening of the frontiers of learning; Sir Henry Savile of Merton in 1619 endowed the Savilian professorships of Astronomy and Geometry, and between 1621 and 1636 chairs were set up for moral philosophy, ancient history, anatomy, music, and Arabic. It was also a period of much building and rebuilding, and many of the colleges today have a markedly Jacobean appearance.

As well as being erudite, King James was a man of discernment; he is credited with commenting on Magdalen Tower as 'the most absolute building in Oxford'. James created two university seats in Parliament in 1604, the Members to be elected by Convocation; but the seats were abolished in 1945.

Charles I and William Laud. The vigorous academic activity maintained under Elizabeth and James I continued in the early years of the reign of Charles I, notably driven on by the energetic William Laud (1573–1645), perhaps the last of the churchmen-statesmen who had been prominent before the Reformation. Laud was scholar, Fellow, and President of St John's College, Chancellor of the University in 1630, and in 1633 Archbishop of Canterbury. He drew up for the King new statutes, known as the Caroline or Laudian Code, designed to enforce strict orthodox Anglicanism throughout the University, to institute an improved system of (oral) examinations to replace the archaic medieval disputations, and to regulate students' behaviour and even their dress.

The Code confirmed the Elizabethan innovation of the Hebdomadal Council and it formally established the office of Vice-Chancellor to be responsible for the day-to-day government of the University in the absence of a no-longer-resident Chancellor. The Code effectively regulated the University for some two hundred years.

St. John's College Canterbury Quad, with a statue of King Charles I

The Civil War. The University was Royalist in the Civil War. When King Charles was forced to leave London he moved the Court to Oxford and maintained the Royalist Army's headquarters here during the years 1642–46. Besides housing the King and all his retinue, the University and colleges gave large sums of money to the King's Exchequer and contributed many valuable pieces of silver to the Royal Mint set up in New Inn Hall. With this occupation of Oxford, serious study in the University came to a standstill, and entries of students and graduations of scholars declined to a trickle.

During these four years King Charles lived at Christ Church, Queen Henrietta Maria at Merton, and the King's nephew Prince Rupert, commander of the royal cavalry, at Magdalen. The other colleges housed court officials, army officers, and innumerable hangers-on; space had also to be found for workshops, arsenals, and store-rooms; the University Parks were filled with the King's artillery and horses.

The Commonwealth. After the King's flight, when Oxford was no longer occupied, normal academic life had to be restored. Parliament in 1647 sent another dreaded Visitation, composed of Puritans, who met with stubborn resistance but nevertheless carried out a thorough purge of the Heads and Fellows who refused to submit to the authority of Parliament.

Oliver Cromwell and other members of the Long Parliament were Cambridge graduates; they respected learning and were more tolerant of the obstinacies of the Oxford dons than were some of the brash Puritan extremists. Cromwell, as Chancellor of Oxford and Protector or dictator of the nation, was able to curb the reforming zeal of the Puritans. By the 1650s the flow of students matriculating and graduating had been restored, and work had been resumed.

Academic posterity has reason to be grateful to Sir Thomas Fairfax, Commander-in-Chief of the Parliamentary Army; after the King's flight from Oxford Fairfax saw the possibility of Puritan excesses in the old Royalist stronghold and he placed a guard on the Bodleian Library.

The Puritan rule yielded a harvest of extraordinary good and sound knowledge in all parts of learning, and many who were wickedly introduced applied themselves to the study of good learning and the practice of virtue; so that when it pleased God to bring King Charles the Second back to his throne he found that University abounding in excellent learning, devoted to duty and obedience, and little inferior to what it was before its desolation. (Edward Hyde, Earl of Clarendon (1609–74) Chancellor of the University 1660–67) from his *History of the Rebellion and Civil Wars in England.* Proceeds from the sale of this work contributed to the cost of the Clarendon Building.)

The Restoration of the Monarchy. There were two more Visitations in 1660 and in 1662, to reverse the Puritan purges and to ensure the observance of the Act of Uniformity – that is, the supremacy of the Anglican Church and the exclusion of Nonconformists – which deprived the University of many eminent dissenting academics. Nevertheless, the Restoration and the years to the end of the century saw notable advances in science, and it was a period of outstanding achievements in architecture.

John Wilkins, an enlightened Parliamentarian, brother-in-law to Oliver Cromwell, was Warden of Wadham College during the Commonwealth and in the early years of the

Restoration; he was an eminent astronomer and scientist, and he encouraged meetings of men who were 'inquisitive in Natural Philosophy'. After the Restoration, Wilkins drew up a scheme for what became in 1662 The Royal Society, founded in London by the Oxford scientists and an equally eminent group from Cambridge.

These years also saw the most brilliant constellation of architects in Oxford's history, including Christopher Wren and Nicholas Hawksmoor, and two talented amateurs, Henry Aldrich, Dean of Christ Church, and George Clarke, Fellow of All Souls, assisted in some degree by members of the Townesend family, skilled Oxford stone-masons. They left a legacy of incomparable buildings, including such additions to the visible University as the Sheldonian Theatre and the Clarendon Building, and some admirable chapels and libraries, as well as Tom Tower.

James II. With the accession in 1685 of the Roman Catholic James II, the 'closet' Papists or 'Crypto-Catholics' became bolder, and Oxford's Anglicans, remembering the religious upheavals of the past century-and-a-half, were fearful of further Visitations. The King did not endear himself to the University; on the contrary, he 'beat his head against the walls of Magdalen' in a futile attempt to impose his own Papist nominee as President of the College. The King, by appointing a Roman Catholic as Dean of Christ Church, greatly upset Oxford, though the statutes of Henry VIII allowed him to do this; but he exceeded his powers by attempting to impose on Magdalen his own candidate as President. Not only was this not allowed by the college statutes, which gave the Fellows the right to elect their President, but moreover the King's nominee was an unqualified and wholly unsuitable person. When the

The Clarendon Building

Fellows of Magdalen objected, the King sent a Commission to expel them, and in 1687 he came in person to reprimand them. However, public opinion all over the country was so antagonized that James later relented and restored the expelled Fellows with the President of their choice; but it was too late for him to save his crown, and in 1688 he was deposed.

William III. The Anglicans of Oxford soon felt themselves threatened again, this time by the Calvinism of William III, who succeeded to the throne in 1689. He antagonized the conservative sentiments of the Anglican Tories, and pleased the reformist Whigs, by encouraging Nonconformist preachers; moreover he demanded from all clergy – who still included the Heads and Fellows of the colleges – an oath of allegiance to the joint sovereigns William and Mary, and the repudiation of Romish doctrines. Fourteen Jacobite Tory dons refused the oath and lost their fellowships. William came to Oxford in 1695, and there were Whigs enough to give him a hospitable welcome, but he was so unsure of their loyalty, or so boorish, that at a banquet prepared in his honour he refused to eat and rudely took himself off.

Queen Anne and John Radcliffe. Oxford welcomed Queen Anne cordially when she came in the year of her accession, 1702, on her way to Bath. As a Stuart and a staunch Anglican she was well liked; and all the more since she attempted no reforms but tried to calm down the antagonisms stirred up by William III. Queen Anne did not confer any notable gifts on the University, but she is remembered for having as her physician one of Oxford's major benefactors: Dr John Radcliffe, who bequeathed to the University his great collection of scientific books, and left money to build the Radcliffe Camera to house them; also the Radcliffe Infirmary for the practice of medicine, and the Radcliffe Observatory, now part of Green College; and he gave University College its second quadrangle.

Statue of John Radcliffe

The Hanoverians. The University was essentially Jacobite in sentiment, and greeted the Hanoverian succession in 1714 with little enthusiasm, though it has been claimed that Oxford was eventually won over by the great charm of George III, contrasting strongly with the vacuity of the Jacobite Pretender. The Georgian reigns, however, produced little to encourage learning or research, and there was a general decline in academic standards.

The Wesley Brothers. Contemporary accounts of Oxford in the 18th century give the impression that the town consisted largely of inns and coffee-houses serving as meeting places for the idle rich. Senior and junior common rooms had not then been instituted, and the coffee-houses provided the social setting enjoyed by the 'smarts'

Against this frivolous and indolent background the figures of John (1703–91) and Charles (1707–88) Wesley stand out in contrast. Both were undergraduates at Christ Church in the 1720s; John later became a Fellow of Lincoln and Charles a Student (Fellow) of Christ Church. In 1729 they formed with friends a group, the 'Holy Club', for the strict and regular observance of the rules and sacraments of the Church; because of their strictness and regularity they came to be known as 'Methodists' and were the founders of the Methodist Church.

Music at Oxford. The Georgian years were not entirely barren, especially in music. Handel spent a week in Oxford in July 1733, when he conducted performances of *Esther* and *Deborah*, and the first performance of his new oratorio *Athalia*, all three in the Sheldonian Theatre; his *Te Deum, Jubilate*, and *Coronation Anthems* in St Mary's Church; and *Acis & Galatea* in the hall at Christ Church. Later Haydn, when he was staying in London in 1791–2, came to Oxford to receive an honorary Doctorate of Music. During his visit his Symphony No 92 was played here and became known as the 'Oxford' Symphony.

The Holywell Music Room was built in 1748 to meet the demand for an adequate concert hall. It is believed that this building, designed specifically for the rehearsal and performance of music, is Europe's oldest purpose-built auditorium of its kind.

Disputations. Up to the 16th century, and even beyond, reading and writing played a minor part in the students' activities; there were few books; teaching was by lectures, and examinations were by disputation – that is, by question and answer or 'logic-chopping'. This system gradually degenerated until by the end of the 18th century it had become meaningless. Written examinations were introduced with the reforms of 1800. A proper system of written degree examinations eventually replaced the medieval disputations which, even though improved by Laud's reforms, had become farcical. After 1808 the new method developed into the Honours Schools of *Literae Humaniores* (the classics, or 'Greats') and of Mathematics; the Faculties of Law, of Modern History, and of Physical Science were included from 1850, when the system now in force was introduced.

The Oxford Movement. In the 1830s among the intellectually eminent Fellows of Oriel College, were John Keble, Thomas Arnold, and John Henry Newman who, supported by Canon Edward Pusey of Christ Church and others, formed a group known as the Oxford Movement, alternatively as the Tractarians, or familiarly as the Puseyites. Not unlike the Wesleys before them, they were disgusted by the indolence prevailing in the Church, and they sought to revive the spirit of early Christianity. Although the Movement faded away after some years; it has a lasting monument in Keble College, founded in 1868 by John Keble's friends after his death. The Oxford Movement earned the name 'Tractarians' by their vigorous output of *Tracts for the Times*, some of which, especially No. XC by Newman, caused a great stir at the time but are not now widely remembered.

Victorian Reforms. The Oxford University Act of 1854, and further reforms in 1871 and 1877, entirely freed the University from the control of the Church of England, did away with all religious obligations, such as formal acceptance of the Thirty-Nine Articles, and made Fellows free to marry and live out of college, and to profess any religion, or none. Also fellowships ceased to be comfortable sinecures and began to entail serious tutorial or research work. The reforms were criticized, however, for abolishing the institution of servitors, which made it even more difficult for indigent students to get into the University. There was no improvement in this respect until 1904 after the Education Act of 1902 had led to a new class of secondary schools with the power to grand university scholarships to promising pupils; even then, progress was considered slow.

Eminent Victorians. The second half of the 19th century saw many notable men in Oxford, among them: the great classical scholar Benjamin Jowett, Master of Balliol; the eccentric Dr W. A. Spooner, Warden of New College; the brilliant John Keble, Professor of Poetry; John Ruskin as Slade Professor of Fine Art; Henry Liddell, Dean of Christ Church, one of the authors of the Liddell and Scott Greek Lexicon, (Robert Scott was at Balliol) and father of *Alice* and her sisters. The Revd Charles L. Dodgson, a modest mathematician Student of Christ Church, under his pen-name of Lewis Carroll became more widely known than any of his erudite contemporaries. Also for the first time eminent women appeared in academic roles in Victorian Oxford; personalities such as Miss Elizabeth Wordsworth of Lady Margaret Hall and Miss Dorothea Beale of St Hilda's.

Women's Colleges. An Association for the Education of Women in Oxford was formed in 1878, and was followed by the founding of four women's colleges and the Society of Home Students. From about 1884 women were allowed (duly chaperoned) to attend university lectures

St Hilda's College

26

and to sit the examinations, and from 1920 they were admitted to full membership of the University and entitled to receive degrees. In 1927 the reactionary male dons succeeded in imposing a limit on the number of women undergraduates to be admitted each year; this restriction was not lifted until 1956.

The women's colleges and the dates of their foundation were: Lady Margaret Hall, 1878; Somerville, 1879; St Hugh's, 1886; St Hilda's, 1893; and the Society of Home Students, 1879, which became St Anne's College in 1952. All acquired full collegiate status in 1959.

The Twentieth Century. The University was profoundly affected by both the World Wars. The enormous loss of lives in 1914–18 severely reduced the undergraduate population, from 1,400 in October 1914 to 369 in 1918, and there was a similar loss of young dons; every college has its Roll of Honour, usually in the chapel or ante-chapel, telling the grim story. The second World War involved a rather less massive loss of lives, and larger numbers of undergraduates returned to their colleges, older and more experienced than when they had left. Their influence led to many reforms, including improvements in the status of women.

Yet another Royal Commission came in 1919–22; one of its crucial recommendations was the granting of state aid to the University, to replace the disappearing endowments of previous centuries. From 1925 the University witnessed a rapid expansion of science teaching and scientific research, and was able to draw on state resources for lectureships, laboratories and specialist libraries. The University's activity in this field became increasingly important after the formal organization in 1945 of state funding through the University Grants Committee.

Modern Benefactors. The outstanding, though not the only, benefactor of 20th-century Oxford was Lord Nuffield, William R. Morris, a man of humble origin who became England's leading motor-car industrialist. and made Oxford one of the country's major manufacturing centres. He founded Nuffield College and made handsome gifts to other colleges, but his major benefactions were to Oxford's medical resources. Other modern benefactors include: M.Antonin Besse (St Antony's College); the Wolfson Foundation (Wolfson College); Mr Richard Blackwell (St Cross College); and Dr Cecil Green, of Texas Instruments, who endowed Green College specifically for medical students.

Other benefactions have led to the setting up of new colleges on the existing foundations of academic institutions. Thus Templeton College and Kellogg College, followed by Mansfield and Harris-Manchester, acquired fully independent status within the University, largely on the basis of their financial solidity.

Later in the 1990s appeared a powerful benefactor, Mr Wafic Said, a Saudi financier, with plans for a business school or management studies centre, to be built on a large vacant site adjoining the railway station. Besides centralizing disseminated studies the building will no doubt improve the visual approach to Oxford from the West.

Also in the late 1990s alarms were sounded at a proposal to build an Islamic study centre, complete with mosque, on the edge of the city near Magdalen, an example of the weakening of cultural and religious barriers.

Later Developments. The 1990s saw an increase in graduate research and in university (as distinct from college) teaching posts, chiefly in the sciences. The college system has consequently absorbed growing numbers of university-appointed professors and lecturers (the so-called 'non-dons') and research graduates, known as Recognized Students.

Since 1981, when the Goverment imposed the first cuts in university funding, there has been anxiety in academic circles about maintaining tutorial standards in the face of declining financial resources and growing student membership. The Education Reform Act of 1988, although it attempted to allay these fears, raised new questions and suspicions by abolishing the University Grants Committee, a purely advisory body, and replacing it with a University Funding Council wielding greater powers of intervention widely seen as threatening the universities' cherished independence.

In 1995 a Commission of Enquiry under the Vice-Chancellor Peter North examined the growing complexity of relations, financial and other, between the University and the colleges, and the increasing strain on the loyalties of teaching staff who work for both the University and a college, the fragmentation of responsibility for admissions, the allocation of resources between teaching and research, and between graduate and undergraduate demands.

Beginning in the 1970s and virtually completed by the 1990s, the most profound social change has been the decision by the men's colleges to elect women Fellows and to admit women as undergraduates, while most of the women's colleges have opened their doors to men.

Central Oxford from the East

Conclusion. The University still dominates the City of Oxford, both economically and architecturally; the old town-and-gown antagonisms have disappeared, and the citizens are no longer subservient to the Chancellor as they were in medieval times; but Oxford nevertheless consists of a university of world pre-eminence occupying a city of secondary importance.

The University is a federal body with faculties, libraries, laboratories, and offices all over the city; there is no single easily identifiable seat of government, no visible senate house, just as there is no campus. The federated colleges, by contrast, are physically prominent and give the town its particular character.

Since 1420 matriculation into the University (enrolment into the student body) has been confined to members of academic halls and colleges; the University in effect ceded to the colleges responsibility for the admission, regulation, and tuition of students. In the Arts and the Higher Faculties the curriculum is drawn up and taught largely by Fellows of colleges; but the colleges have no power to confer degrees, which is the prerogative of the University.

In the Arts, resources may be obtained by the exercise of pressure on governments and on private trusts and foundations, but money often runs short of academic ambition. In the Sciences there are more promising sources to be tapped; there is increased collaboration between the university laboratories and manufacturing corporations. Such developments as these, though encouraging for the scientists, are unlikely to result in profound changes in the structure and nature of the University and its score of faculties.

At Magdalen Bridge

ITINERARIES

The central and oldest part of the City of Oxford, containing the buildings of major historical or architectural importance, is here described in three notional walks intended as a help to visitors in finding their way about this rather tortuous town. These three walks begin and end within a few metres of Blackwell's Bookshop in The Broad,which is easy to find and to recognize. The following pages contain a few historical notes by way of background to the buildings.

Many of the college chapels and halls are worth visiting for their architecture, interior woodwork, stained glass, and portraits of Founders, Heads, and other notables; many of the college gardens are enchanting. However, it must be noted that the several university institutions and the colleges observe no unified timetable and each of them is open or closed to the public as it sees fit. Visitors are advised to enquire by telephone.

Buildings here mentioned under headings in italics either are not open to the public or cannot usefully be visited as part of an itinerary; they are included for their architectural or historical interest. The principal museums are briefly noticed for the benefit of visitors with time to spare.

References to *Pevsner* are to the volume *Oxfordshire* by Jennifer Sherwood and Nikolaus Pevsner in *The Buildings of England* series by Penguin Books.

Blackwell's in The Broad

ITINERARY I

Sheldonian Theatre. Across Broad Street (The Broad) from Blackwell's Bookshop stands a row of carved stone heads, commonly called 'Emperors' or 'Caesars'. Beyond them is the Sheldonian Theatre, built as a ceremonial assembly hall for occasions such as the annual *Encaenia*, degree-giving, and the like. It is one of the principal buildings of the University.

Gilbert Sheldon, Archbishop of Canterbury, Chancellor, and former Warden of All Souls College, in 1663 commissioned Christopher Wren – Savilian Professor of Astronomy and a Fellow of All Souls – to design a hall suitable for university ceremonies and commemorations. These were then currently held in St Mary's Church but had become too rowdy, especially the annual rumpus known as 'The Act', the ancient annual degree-giving, speech-making,

The Sheldonian Theatre

verse-reciting event, which by the middle of the 17th century had become a rowdy celebration with bawdy orations by the *Terrae Filius* – a sort of licensed jester – and political or even subversive undertones that Church and State regarded with suspicion. Today's impeccably sedate *Encaenia* is derived from 'The Act', but bears little resemblance to it.

Because of its ceremonial purposes the theatre was built with its front facing the Divinity School, also used for ceremonies, and its curved back towards the street. (The visitors' entrance is on the east side, on the left when approached from The Broad). The shape of the building was determined by Wren's design based on an open-air Roman theatre. In pursuit of the open-air illusion and with the collaboration of his friend John Wallis, Savilian Professor of Geometry, he designed a self-supporting ceiling measuring 80 feet by 70 feet (24m x 21m), the greatest flat span then known. Robert Streater, who painted the allegorical happenings on the ceiling, was Sergeant Painter to the King. The work was carried out in Streater's London studio in 1668–9 on thirty-two canvas panels, and brought to Oxford by Thames barge. This ceiling depicts the sky with a simulation of the ropes that in a Roman theatre would have borne a canopy to shade the audience. Streater shows the canopy pulled back by winged cherubs to reveal an allegorical scene in the sky, with Truth descending among the Arts and Sciences to drive out Envy, Rapine, and Ignorance.

In the centre of the gilded auditorium is the Chancellor's throne; at the sides are the two Proctors' boxes ornamented with projecting *fasces* symbolizing proctorial authority.

The theatre, from its opening in 1669 until 1713, housed the incipient Oxford University Press, which occupied spare spaces such as the basement, the rooms beneath the auditorium, and the roof space, then amply lit by the oval dormer windows of Wren's original design. During these years, and for some years following, when the Press was housed in the Clarendon Building, the imprint of the Oxford University Press was *E Theatro Sheldoniano*. In 1802 the roof was rebuilt without the dormers, and in 1838 Wren's lantern was replaced with a larger and heavier-looking design by Edward Blore. The Sheldonian has seldom been used as a theatre for drama but has regularly served as a concert hall.

On the west side of the building the stairs lead up to the roof space, which once housed the typesetters of the University Press, and to the lantern or cupola at the top, which commands good views of the surrounding buildings. Returning to ground level, a walk round the outside of the theatre, clockwise

Sheldonian Theatre: The Chancellor's Throne

beginning at the door on the east side, leads first to the flat front of the building, ordinary neo-classical of Wren's immaturity; the doors in this front are opened on ceremonial occasions, as are those of the Divinity School facing the theatre across the yard. Along the west side of the theatre, returning towards The Broad, there is another narrow yard and a fine doorway in Renaissance style, built surprisingly close. This is the original principal entrance (no longer used) of the Old Ashmolean building, now entered from The Broad.

The seventeen carved stone heads along The Broad are neither Emperors, nor Caesars, nor Apostles, nor even Philosophers; they are reliably said to be part of Wren's Roman Concept and to echo the 'herms' or boundary stones in Rome which were often decorated with carved heads. The original heads at the Sheldonian became badly eroded and were replaced in 1867; these later heads in turn decayed, and new heads by the Oxford sculptor Michael Black were put up in 1972.

Old Ashmolean Museum. Built 1678–83 by Master-mason Thomas Wood. This building was designed to exhibit the antiquities, curiosities, and works of art given to the University by Elias Ashmole (1617–92), who had inherited the collection from John Tradescant the Younger. The exhibits were openly displayed and the Ashmolean became in 1685 the first public museum in England. The building also housed the School of Natural History and England's first chemical laboratory. Ashmole's collection was moved in the 1850s, the art objects to the University Galleries or New Ashmolean in Beaumont Street, and the scientific items to the University Museum. The exhibition of ancient scientific instruments was set up in 1924 on the top floor of the Old Ashmolean, and the basement continued in use as a laboratory.

After the removal of Ashmole's exhibits the building was used to house the Lewis Evans collection of scientific instruments, enlarged by later acquisitions such as the astronomy equipment from the Radcliffe Observatory. Today, it is claimed, the *Museum of the History of Science*, as it is now called, includes the world's finest assembly of astronomical instruments, together with an extensive collection of equipment from the past in the fields of mathematics, medicine, pharmacology, chemistry, photography, and almost every branch of science.

Besides the intrinsic interest of the exhibits there is the additional attraction of a most elegant building, including a magnificent oak staircase.

Clarendon Building. To the east of the Sheldonian stands the dignified *Clarendon Building*, designed by Nicholas Hawksmoor and built in 1711–13 in memory of the Earl of Clarendon, as new premises for the Oxford University Press, which was outgrowing its confined space in the Sheldonian.

The building was in part financed with the proceeds of the eminently successful *History of the Rebellion* by Edward Hyde, first Earl of Clarendon (1609–74), Chancellor of the University 1660–67; there is a statue of him in a niche on the west front facing the Sheldonian. The *History* was published posthumously in 1702–4, and the second Earl made over the copyright and the proceeds to the University. Hawksmoor's design for the building is said to be based on a sketch by Vanbrugh, with whom he was at the time (1710) working at Blenheim Palace,

Old Schools Quad frontispiece with Lesueur's bronze of the Third Earl of Pembroke

Woodstock. The Oxford University Press has retained, and still uses, the *Clarendon Press* imprint, and the Delegates of the Press (the equivalent of Directors) still meet in an elegant room in the south-west corner of the building. When the Press moved again in 1830 to Walton Street the Clarendon Building was given over to university offices. Through the building there is a central passage-way, with fine wrought-iron gates, which is in line with the entrance to the Old Schools Quadrangle.

Old Schools Quadrangle – Bodleian Library. The buildings that form the quadrangle date from 1610–24; they were planned by Sir Thomas Bodley as part of his grand library scheme. The top floor was intended for the expansion of the library and the lower floors were for the lecture rooms and examination halls of the various 'schools', identified by the names above the doors. They were arranged, in relation to the main gate, in the same order as was prescribed for students following the Trivium and the Quadrivium, which together made the seven-year Arts course. The buildings are now wholly occupied by the library.

Architecturally the Old Schools Quad is austere except for its main gateway in the east range; this is ornamented with a five-tier frontispiece exemplifying the five orders of classical architecture: At the fourth level the statuary represents King James I giving his works to the University, on his left, and to Fame, with her trumpet. *Pevsner* says: '... such a frontispiece will never be seen again. With five tiers it is the biggest in England, and that means anywhere'.

The west range of the Quad is filled by the Proscholium or ante-chamber of the Divinity School, with a wing of Duke Humfrey's Library above it. The entrance is behind Hubert Lesueur's bronze statue of the Third Earl of Pembroke, who was Chancellor when the Quad was being built, and was one of the Library's benefactors.

Divinity School. The main structure of this building was begun in the early 1400s, but the decorated vaulting was not completed until about 1480; it is said to be one of the finest examples of English perpendicular, and is the work of the stone-mason William Orchard.

The hall of the Divinity School was primarily used for oral examinations, or disputations, for the degree of Doctor of Divinity, the highest academic distinction of the middle ages; hence it was the most splendid of the many examination halls that originally formed the Schools Quad, and it is the only one to survive virtually unchanged, except for the addition of Wren's ceremonial 'Gothick' doorway facing the Sheldonian. Beyond the hall at its far end, but not normally open to the public, is the *Convocation House* of 1640 where the university 'parliament' meets.

The Divinity School

Duke Humfrey's Library. The upper floor above the Divinity School is the library built to house the books and manuscripts given to the University by Humfrey Duke of Gloucester, younger brother of Henry V. The library was opened in 1488, was destroyed in 1549 by the rapacious Puritan commissioners of the Visitation sent by Edward VI, and was restored in 1602 as the centre of Sir Thomas Bodley's great library, which now fully occupies the buildings that form the Old Schools Quad. Not long afterwards, in 1610, Bodley added the transverse wing known as the Arts End, with the Divinity School Proscholium on the ground floor. In 1636–40 Archbishop Laud added the Convocation House, with the Seldon End of the Library above it, as a balancing transverse wing at the western end of the building.

Duke Humfrey's Library is not publicly accessible, though it can be viewed from the Arts End, which is occasionally open to visitors. Enquiries may be made in the Proscholium. (01865) 277000.

Back in the Old Schools Quad; in the south range there is a passage-way leading into Radcliffe Square.

Radcliffe Camera, (built 1737–49) The circular classical building in the centre of the square is one of Oxford's most notable features; *Pevsner* describes it as 'England's most accomplished domed building'. Dr John Radcliffe, physician to Queen Anne, bequeathed his great collection of scientific books to the University, with money for a building to house them. The idea of a rotunda originated with Hawksmoor, but he died in 1736 and the final design was by James Gibbs. Dr Radcliffe's books are now in the Radcliffe Science Library and the Camera has become the principal reading room of the Bodleian Library.

The south side of Radcliffe Square is wholly taken up by St Mary's Church, which has one entrance on the square and another on the High Street.

St Mary the Virgin, The University Church. The huge tower of St Mary's dominates Radcliffe Square, and indeed the whole of Oxford; historically St Mary's is the most important building in the city. There has been a parish church on this site since the 11th-century; in the very earliest days of the University the church was used for academic disputations, religious trials of heretics, secular university ceremonies and celebrations, and the day-to-day business of the body of Masters.

St Mary's is where the burgesses were humiliated by the Church after the 1354 riots, and where the three Protestant Bishops were tried and condemned to be burned at the stake for heresy. Queen Elizabeth I attended a series of academic disputations at St Mary's in 1566, accompanied by the Earl of Leicester, whose wife Amy Robsart had been buried at the western end of the nave after dying mysteriously at Cumnor. John Henry Newman was vicar of St Mary's, 1828–43, before he 'went over to Rome' and became a Cardinal.

The massive tower was built onto the 11th-century nave about 1280, and the spire was added some forty years later, around 1320. In the following century the choir and the nave were rebuilt between 1460 and 1490 and are, with some modifications, what stands today. The baroque portico on the High Street by Nicholas Stone and most of the interior woodwork are of the 17th century; the amusing gargoyles round the top of the tower, below the spire, were added in the restoration of 1892–96. The huge statues on the tower are 19th-century copies of the originals.

The Radcliffe Camera from Exeter College Fellows' Garden

St Mary's Church from The High

The tower is normally open to visitors for a modest fee; there are vast views from the top.

Adjacent to the church is a small two-storey hall known as the *Old Congregation House*, built in 1320; it is the first building owned by the University, and for about a century was the only one. The lower floor was used as a council chamber until 1640, (when the Convocation House was built adjoining the Divinity School); the upper floor housed the university library until Duke Humfrey's Library was opened in the 1480s.

In this upper room in 1942 the Oxford Committee for Famine Relief was constituted, and *Oxfam* came into existence.

Leaving St Mary's by the south door with its baroque portico on the High Street, a left turn leads across Catte Street to All Souls College.

All Souls College, High Street. Founded 1438 by Archbishop Chichele, as The Warden and College of the Souls of all Faithful People deceased in the University of Oxford.

The foundation was by Henry Chichele, Archbishop of Canterbury, with the support of King Henry VI; it was finally named The College of All Souls of the Faithful Departed and was intended as a chantry where prayers were to be constantly said for the souls of all those who had died in the Hundred Years War against France. The founder intended also that the college should produce competent administrators for Church and State, and his statutes required that the forty members of the college, with preference for his kin, should be Masters intending to proceed to doctorates. The college has not changed its original principles and still does not admit undergraduate members; the Fellows are all eminent graduates of Oxford or other universities.

The statues on the gate-tower are of the founders, Archbishop Chichele and Henry VI, and the carved relief depicts the Resurrection; all three are 1939 replacements.

The small front quad, entered from The High, dates from the foundation and is little altered; the north range, facing the gatehouse is occupied by the chapel, which is T-shaped like the chapels of Merton and New College; the entrance is on the left in the west range. The ornate screen in the chapel is of 1664, remodelled in 1716; the impressive reredos is basically contemporary with the building, 1447, but the original figures were damaged during the Reformation, and in the 17th-century it was all plastered up and covered with a seemingly crude painting of the Resurrection, 'too full of nakeds' for the sober taste of John Evelyn the diarist.

All Souls, The Hawksmoor Towers

The plaster was removed and the figures were restored in the 1870s. In the choir stalls are some exquisitely carved 15th-century misericords.

In the north-east corner of the Front Quad a passage leads into the North Quad, designed by Nicholas Hawksmoor in consultation with the Warden Dr George Clarke. This large quad was built in 1714–34 on the site of an old cloister; its dominant feature is Hawksmoor's characteristic pair of Gothic towers. On the far side of the quad is his Codrington Library, equally Gothic externally but Palladian classical inside. The sundial on the wall of the library was originally designed for the Front Quad by Christopher Wren when he was Bursar of the college. This North Quad is the more attractive for having its west side open, with only a low arcade, allowing an excellent view of the Radcliffe Camera, which Hawksmoor knew about when he was building his quad, though work on the Camera did not begin until 1737, the year after his death.

The old hall was demolished and a larger one was built by Dr Clarke and Hawksmoor, resulting in the formation of a corner to the east of the Front Quad, known as Hall Quad, like a small garden. A notable adjunct to the hall is the vaulted buttery, much admired by Sir Hugh Casson. To the east and on The High is the Warden's Lodging, designed by Warden Clarke for himself in 1706 and said by *Pevsner* to be 'the first piece of Palladianism in Oxford and probably in England'. On the other side of the Warden's Garden is the Manciple's House, late 16th-century. A right turn out of All Souls main gate in The High leads back to Catte Street, which goes into Radcliffe Square again. Facing All Souls across the square is Brasenose College.

41

Brasenose College ('BNC') Radcliffe Square. Founded 1509 by William Smyth, Bishop of Lincoln, and Sir Richard Sutton as The Principal and Scholars of the King's Hall and College of Brasenose in Oxford.

'BNC' occupies the west side of Radcliffe Square; it stands on the sites of several medieval halls, including Brazen Nose Hall, so called for a brass door knocker or sanctuary ring in the shape of an animal face, said to be of the 12th century, that adorned its main gate. The college was endowed and founded in 1509 by William Smyth, Bishop of Lincoln (the diocese then included Oxford) and Sir Richard Sutton, a lawyer, both natives of Lancashire.

The Old Quad, the first entered from the gateway, is contemporary with the foundation, except that the gable dormer windows were added a century later when a third storey was made in the attics; the fine gate-tower was originally (as was the custom) the Principal's Lodging, and now is so again in preference to the noisier lodgings on the High Street. The sundial on the north range dates from 1719. The hall, seen from the gatehouse, is on the left of the quad; inside, on the wall above the high table, the original Brazen Nose is displayed, with other works of art. In the migration to Stamford, Lincolnshire, in 1334 some of the scholars took the knocker with them. It remained there for five centuries and was recovered by the college only in 1890, leaving its name in a corner of Stamford.

To the south the small Chapel Quad of 1664 has an unusual arcade leading to a fine baroque chapel with decorated plaster vaulting. The heavy screen and organ case are late 19th-century. Beyond the chapel is the larger New Quad of 1909, by Thomas G. Jackson, its rather dull High Street front enlivened by grotesque and amusing carvings. To the west of this quad, fitted into a small space, is a modern concrete residential pill-box.

A left turn out of the main gate of BNC leads to Brasenose Lane, with its medieval kennel or gutter down the centre, below a high wall concealing the Fellows' Garden of Exeter College. The lane leads to Turl Street ('The Turl') and the Covered Market, to be seen later in this itinerary.

Back across the square, continuing along Catte Street with the Old Schools building on the left, is Hertford College on the right.

Hertford College, Catte Street. Founded 1283 as Hart Hall by Elias de Hertford; refounded 1740, 1822, 1874 by successive benefactors as the Principal, Fellows and Scholars of Hertford College in the University of Oxford.

The history of Hertford begins with Hart Hall of the 1280s, and continues with several changes of ownership and of name during its long and rather precarious existence. From 1312 it belonged to Walter de Stapledon, Bishop of Exeter, who set up his first community of scholars here and renamed it Stapledon Hall; when in 1314 he moved his scholars to St Stephen's Hall, later Exeter College, Hart Hall reverted to its old name and continued as an academic hall in the ownership of Exeter. In 1740 the vigorous Principal, Dr Richard Newton, refounded the hall as Hertford College, but he was not able to arrange adequate endowments and the college was poor from the beginning. Its fortunes declined further and by 1805 there were no students and only two Fellows; in 1818 it was closed. From 1822 the buildings were occupied by Magdalen Hall and were so named. The hall prospered, and another energetic Principal, with a benefaction from the banker Thomas Baring, refounded it in 1874 under its earlier name of Hertford College.

Brasenose College High Street Front with St Mary's Church

The Palladian Catte Street front was built in 1822 by Magdalen Hall to replace a medieval block that had collapsed. Inside, most of the front quad was rebuilt by Thomas G. Jackson in the 1880s with an admirable 'French Renaissance' stair tower up to the hall; in the south range there are two chapels – one of 1716, now the library, and one of 1908. The east range, opposite the gate, contains the only surviving part of the medieval Hart Hall.

In 1898 the college acquired land on the north side of New College Lane, where the North Quad was built round an octagonal chapel of about 1520. The 'Bridge of Sighs' by Jackson (inspired by Contino) was built in 1914 to connect the two quads. A recent enlargement of the college is the new Holywell Quad on Holywell Street, where modern buildings have been combined with old houses.

On the north side of New College Lane there is a house where the astronomer Edmund Halley lived and worked in the early years of the 18th century, and where he built a private observatory. In his long and eminent career his scientific work was by no means confined to comets, yet he is best known for his observation of the 1682 comet that now bears his name; he identified it as being the same as the comet recorded in 1531 and 1607, and he accurately predicted its reappearance in 1758–9.

Hertford College: 'Bridge of Sighs'

Near-by is a narrow opening, St Helen's Passage (or 'Hell Passage'), which leads tortuously to the 'Turf Tavern' in the centre of the labyrinth, and beyond to Bath Place, which gives onto Holywell Street opposite the *Holywell Music Room*. This concert hall, opened in 1748, was designed and built specifically for the performance of music, and is said to be the world's oldest such building. It is owned by Wadham College.

From beneath the 'Bridge of Sighs' New College Lane leads to New College's principal gate.

New College, New College Lane and Holywell Street. Founded 1379 by William of Wykeham as St Mary College of Winchester in Oxford.

William of Wykeham (1323–1404), Bishop of Winchester, was a rich and powerful prelate who enjoyed royal patronage. His foundation soon became known as 'New College' to distinguish it from the older House of Blessed Mary the Virgin in Oxford, founded in 1326, known as Oriel. William of Wykeham, as other founders before him, intended his college to produce erudite clerks to be administrators of Church and State, or to teach others; he also introduced new principles into the scheme of university education, thus earning his college the name of 'new' in more than the temporal sense. To ensure a supply of students adequately

New College Garden Quad.

Epstein's Lazarus

versed in Latin, he founded his school in Winchester, which for many years was the only source of scholars, ultimately of Fellows, at New College. He also ordained that students were to live in the college – rather than in halls as was then customary – and that the whole university curriculum should be taught in the college by the body of resident Masters. These innovations were reflected in the founder's detailed planning of the college buildings, where he exercised his knowledge of practical architecture acquired when he was Surveyor of the Royal Castles.

The Great Quad is today much as William of Wykeham built it about 1385, except for the third storey added in 1647. The north range is occupied by the huge chapel and proportionately large hall; the Muniment Tower, of four storeys, is in the north-east corner of the quad, and the library is in the upper part of most of the east range.

The chapel ranks with that of Merton as one of Oxford's finest and, like Merton's, it is T-shaped. The ante-chapel contains a wealth of original 14th-century glass in the transept windows. The great west window is contrastingly filled with glass designed by Joshua Reynolds, 1785, depicting the Seven Virtues and a Nativity; Reynolds himself did not consider the work a great success, and certainly the style and the colouring are very different from those of the surrounding glass. Below this west window stands Epstein's intense sculpture *Lazarus*, of 1951. On the east wall of the ante-chapel, near the war-memorial plaque, are inscribed the names of three German members of the college who died in the First World War, with sensitive wording, attributed to Warden W.A.Spooner (1903-24).

> *In memory of the men of this college who coming*
> *from a foreign land entered into the inheritance*
> *of this place and returning fought and died for*
> *their country in the war 1914–1919.*

The choir is reached through a heavy screen surmounted by a very advanced organ installed in 1969. The elaborate reredos is a 19th-century reconstruction of an original destroyed during the Reformation. The woodwork is also rebuilt, but many fine 14th-century misericords and elbow-rests have been incorporated. The glass in the side-windows of the choir is unremarkable 18th-century.

On the north wall near the vestry door is a painting of an Apostle, said to be St James, by El Greco; nearer the altar a glassed-in recess contains William of Wykeham's silver-gilt crozier. 'The most magnificent example of later 14th-century goldsmiths' work in Great Britain' in the words of *Pevsner*.

West of the chapel, to the right out of the door, through a short tunnel-like passage, is the cloister, originally a burial ground. Not overlooked by any inhabited building and leading nowhere, it is a silent haven in the centre of the noisy city, dominated by the 14th-century bell-tower and an immense holm-oak. The ancient statues against the walls are some of those taken down from the tower of St Mary's church in the 1890s.

Returning to the Great Quad: the stone stairs in the north-east corner under the Muniment Tower lead up to the hall, which is large and rather dark; the medieval-looking smoke-louvre in the roof is part of the reconstruction of 1865. The screen and the linen-fold panelling, however, are 16th-century. In the screen passage one of the smaller doorways leading to the buttery and pantry has in its spandrels amusing carvings of boys, perhaps choristers, carrying beer and bread. In the hall itself there is a good collection of portraits, beginning with that of the Founder and including one of the celebrated and eccentric. Spooner, whose peculiarities of speech – 'spoonerisms' and other oddities – concealed a lucid mind. The ground floor of the Muniment Tower, beside the hall steps, contains the college silver and other treasures including *perhaps* a unicorn's horn.

The archway in the east range of the Great Quad leads into the Garden Quad, built in several stages between 1450 and 1718; the buildings of this last stage have the earliest recorded example of sash-windows in Oxford. The Garden Quad is open on its east side and is separated from the garden itself by a magnificent wrought-iron screen of 1711.

The spacious garden reveals at once how New College was built by the founder close to the city wall, the only available site inside the city large enough for his plans. To this day the college is responsible for the maintenance of the wall within its territory. The mound in the garden was made in 1594 and later improved with the addition of steps. To the south-east, about a quarter of a mile away, Magdalen Tower appears among the trees, and close at hand to

View from the Great Quad, New College

the south is the tower of St Peter-in-the-East (*see St Edmund Hall.*)

New College is well known for its excellent choir; the college maintains in Savile Road a boys' school, from which choristers are drawn.

Leaving New College by its Holywell gate and turning right in this admirable street of 17th and 18th-century houses, leads in a hundred yards or so to Longwall Street, which curves round to the right. On the curve is a red-brick building, now belonging to New College, where in 1912 W. R. Morris (Lord Nuffield) began producing his Morris-Oxford Light Car. Alternatively, return to the main entrance then back under the 'Bridge of Sighs' and enter Holywell Street at its intersection with The Broad and Catte Street.

Longwall Street ends at The High; to the left, on the other side of the long wall is Magdalen College, identified by its magnificent bell-tower.

Magdalen College, High Street. Founded in 1458 by William of Wayneflete as The President and Scholars of the College of St Mary Magdalen in the University of Oxford.

Wayneflete (1395–1486) was another powerful churchman who followed the Wykehamist path to eminence. He began as a scholar at Winchester, went on to New College, returned to Winchester as Headmaster, later became first Provost of Eton College (founded by Henry VI), then Bishop of Winchester and Lord Chancellor to Henry VI, whose patronage he put to good use.

The Hospital of St John the Baptist, though it was almost derelict and had only a handful of monks living in it, owned extensive lands in Oxford and had a large income. Wayneflete obtained Royal and Papal authority to suppress the hospital and appropriate its lands, buildings and revenues to his foundation, which consequently began its life with ample endowments. The Hospital stood outside the East Gate of the city on the banks of the Cherwell. Here Wayneflete founded Magdalen College in 1458, and it was generously funded, though it did not become an effective community until about 1480.

Building at the hospital site was delayed by the beginning of the Wars of the Roses and the defeat of Wayneflete's patron Henry VI. However, not only was Wayneflete a man of determination, but also he lived to the age of 90, and he saw the completion of all his buildings except the bell-tower.

Magdalen attracted many benefactions and soon became the richest college in Oxford; by the end of the 15th-century it was among the leaders of the 'new learning', with several eminent classical Humanists among its Fellows and Demies. (A Demi was a scholar receiving half the allowance of a Fellow; today the name is applied to undergraduate scholars. *See Postmasters* at Merton). In the 17th-century Magdalen's quarrel with James II over the nomination of a President contributed to the downfall of that disliked monarch.

The buildings of Magdalen are much embellished with grotesque and humorous carvings, both ancient and modern; many are portraits, or rather caricatures, of Fellows, bursars, surveyors, and stone-masons. Inside the cloister there is an abundance of older figures including monsters, allegories and stone-carvers' fantasies.

The bell-tower, built in 1492–1509 in the purest Perpendicular style, under the guidance of William Orchard, restored in 1980–81, is one of Oxford's architectural treasures; it is 144 feet (44 meters) in height and hung in it are ten melodious bells of various dates from the 15th century to the 18th. At dawn on May Day the college choir assembles at the top of the tower and sings to expectant crowds below.

Magdalen College Bell-Tower and The Cherwell

An ornamental 19th-century gateway – not in use as an entrance – leads into St John's Quad, named for the medieval hospital on the site. The east range on the right consists of the west front of the chapel, the Muniment Tower, and the Founder's Tower (the original gatehouse), all built between 1474 and 1488. In the south-east corner of this quad there is a stone pulpit from which an open-air sermon was formerly preached on the feast of St John the Baptist. In the diagonally opposite corner a modest old-looking building stands alone; it dates from 1614 and is the only surviving part of the Grammar Hall, which Wayneflete set up to prepare boys in Latin for further studies in the college.

The chapel, built in 1474–80, follows the T-plan of Merton and New College, and it has elegant slender piers at the crossing. The ante-chapel is darkened by the rather murky painted glass of the 1630s, but is lofty and has a fine west window. The stone screen into the choir, the stone reredos, and the woodwork in the choir, are the work of the architect L. Cottingham, who carried out the restoration of 1829–34. The old stalls to be seen in the ante-chapel are thought to have been in the choir before the restoration work; they are decorated with some interesting misericords.

A right turn out of the chapel leads into the 15th-century cloister, which is the centre of the college; the hall is entered from it; rooms open off it; and it has doorways into the gardens and to the New Buildings. To the right goes direct to the hall (1475), which is in line with the chapel as at New College; here too the hall is built on the upper floor and is approached up steps. The linen-fold panelling is 15th-century, and the Elizabethan screen of 1600 is said to be the finest in Oxford. At the high-table end of the hall are some interesting carved panels, dated 1541, portraying Henry VIII and incidents in the life of St Mary Magdalene. In the hall is a

Magdalen College cloister

portrait of the most remarkable of Presidents: Martin Routh, who was elected a Fellow in 1775 at the age of twenty, at thirty-five became President, and continued in this office until he died in his hundredth year in 1854; he was the last man in Oxford to wear a wig, and his many eccentricities made him appear never to have emerged from the 18th century.

From the hall to the opposite range of the cloister, going clockwise, leads past the Founder's Tower to a passage into the gardens, which on the far side have the stately classical New Buildings of 1733 (attributed to Dr George Clarke and James Gibbs) standing away from the nucleus of the college, surrounded by gardens and riverside walks.

From St John's Quad, Chaplain's Yard is approached through a passage beneath the stone pulpit. The yard is formed by the south side of the Chapel, the bell tower and the backs of the 16th-century buildings that face onto The High. In the other direction, west of St John's Quad and south of the old Grammar Hall, are St Swithun's and Longwall Quads formed by 19th and 20th-century buildings, including the New Library of 1851.

To the north of this group, along the inner side of the long wall, the college has contrived an ambitious extension of student living quarters and a theatre. It is an arrangement of buildings designed by Demetri Porphyrios that harmonize well with the earlier parts of the college.

Besides being rich, Magdalen was set up in open land outside the city, and could command space to become the most extensive of all the college foundations. Magdalen now owns more than a hundred acres (forty hectares) of riverside walks and meadows, including Addison's Walk and other Civil War earthworks, and The Grove, a deer park that has had deer in it since the late 17th century. Outside the college site Magdalen owns a 1935 annexe in Longwall Street, and the Wayneflete Building of 1960 across Magdalen Bridge, a dull building with a shopping arcade on the ground floor.

Magdalen, the deer park

Magdalen School and Magdalen Hall. Alongside his College Wayneflete set up a Grammar School to prepare boys for the university course; this school later branched out into Magdalen Hall, a home for indigent scholars who could not afford to enter the College. It grew into one of the larger and more successful academic halls; but Magdalen Hall and Magdalen College were uneasy neighbours, and when in 1820 the Hall buildings were destroyed by fire there was a welcome opportunity for its members to move into the empty buildings of the closed-down Hart Hall (Hertford College). The Grammar School moved too, but returned to its old site when a new schoolroom was built in the college grounds in 1851; this building is now the college library on the corner of Longwall Street. Since 1894 the School has occupied its own site on the far bank of the Cherwell.

Magdalen Bridge. There has been a bridge at this point since the 11th century; the present structure by John Gwynn was built in 1772–82, widened in 1882, and restored in the 1990s. In the shadow of the bridge, almost adjoining the college, there is a boat station with punts for hire.

Across Magdalen Bridge is a traffic maelstrom called The Plain, once a village green; leading out of the roundabout, clockwise, are St Clement's Street, which goes past Magdalen's Florey Building (1970). Cowley Road, Iffley Road, and Cowley Place. This last is a cul-de-sac ending at the gates of St Hilda's College beyond the buildings of Magdalen College School.

Magdalen College School and The Cherwell

St Hilda's College, Cowley Place. The College was founded as a women's hall in 1893 by Miss Dorothea Beale, the Principal of Cheltenham Ladies' College.

She bought Cowley House, built in the late 18th century on a fine site overlooking the River Cherwell, and she appointed as first Principal her Cheltenham colleague Mrs Esther Burrows. Over the years buildings have been added and adjoining properties acquired; seven or eight different architects have contributed to the diversity of St

St Hilda's College

Hilda's, and it is now an extensive place making the most of its excellent riverside position; it has had its own boathouse and punts since soon after its foundation. St Hilda's acquired full college status with the other women's colleges in 1959.

Bartlemas. For adventurous visitors the Cowley Road leads in about a mile from The Plain to Bartlemas, or St Bartholomew's Hospital. It lies at the end of an unmade lane off the Cowley Road opposite the large red-brick Bingo hall, former cinema.

Bartlemas was founded for lepers in 1126 by Henry I, and built at a discreet distance from the city. In 1329 the hospital was acquired by Oriel College, and the primitive medieval chapel was rebuilt in the same year. As leprosy declined Bartlemas became increasingly a place of pilgrimage, especially for the health-giving waters of its holy well. The hospital buildings were used for retreats by the Fellows of Oriel.

In the Civil War the Parliamentarians left the chapel unharmed but they destroyed all the other buildings – the almshouses, the Warden's lodging, and the farmhouse – which were rebuilt in the 1650s. These handsome buildings have passed into private ownership, but the ancient chapel and the present-day gardens may be seen and admired.

The return across Magdalen Bridge, on the south side of the road, leads to the Botanic Garden, a haven of quiet after the High Street.

The Botanic Garden, High Street. The 'Physick Garden' as it was first called, facing Magdalen across The High, is not large but it contains trees and plants from all over the world. In 1621 Henry Danvers, Earl of Danby, acquired from Magdalen a derelict plot of land that in the 13th century had been a Jewish cemetery, where he set up a *herbarium* for the Faculty of Medicine. He built the wall and the three gateways, designed by Nicholas Stone, and he endowed the garden with a keeper, a German, Jacob Bobart, who made a vast collection of European and other plants. One of his successors, following his example, brought from the slopes of Mount Etna the plant that became known as 'Oxford Ragwort'. It escaped from the Garden and spread all over England. Bobart's son and successor, also Jacob, raised a hybrid *Platanus* which became the ancestor of the London plane tree.

Academic interest in botany increased rapidly, and in 1669 Charles II created a Professorship of Botany; by the beginning of the 19th century medicine and botany were separate sciences. Charles Daubeny, a Darwinian evolutionist appointed Professor in 1834, changed the name of the garden and the orientation of the research work away from medicine and towards botany and evolution. At his own expense he built the Daubeny Laboratory in 1848. Professor Daubeny was chairman of the famous debate on Darwin's theories that was held at the University Museum in 1860. After the resounding triumph of Thomas Huxley over Bishop

The Botanic Garden

54

Samuel Wilberforce, Daubeny arranged a celebratory party at the Botanic Garden.[4] *(see also University Museum).*

The Garden now extends beyond its south wall into a less formal part with many exotic and mountain plants and a water garden; outside the east wall, facing the Cherwell, are glass-houses containing tropical and sub-tropical 'economic' plants and many rarities.

The cemetery had been in use from about 1190 until 1290, when the Jews were expelled from England. It was approached from the Great Jewry, in what is now St Aldate's and neighbouring streets, by a path that skirted the city wall; a stretch of this path below the wall at Merton is still known as Dead Man's Walk, supposedly from the Jewish funeral processions.

This itinerary now returns westwards in The High on the same side of the street as the Botanic Garden. To the west of the Garden is Rose Lane, which goes to Merton Fields, Dead

Botanic Garden Gateway

Man's Walk, and Christ Church Meadow. Straight on up The High leads to the eastern end of Merton Street, with the Eastgate Hotel on one corner and the Examination Schools on the other side. The building at No 74 High Street houses the *Ruskin School of Drawing and Fine Art*, founded by John Ruskin in 1871 when he was Slade Professor. The school was first set up in the Ashmolean Museum and moved to its present premises in 1975, where it prepares students for the practical work in the Bachelor of Fine Art degree course.

The Examination Schools, High Street. (Opened 1882) This Elizabethan-Jacobean country mansion by Thomas G. Jackson was commissioned when the Old Schools were no longer adequate for the increasing activity in lectures and examinations; from the 1850s examinations were written and took up more time and room than the earlier oral disputations. Visitors may normally look inside the building during vacations.

A hundred yards farther up The High, on the same side of the street, is Logic Lane, and seventy-five yards beyond that is the entrance to University College.

University College, High Street. Founded 1249 by William of Durham as the Master and Fellows of the College of the Great Hall of the University in the University of Oxford.

'Univ' is one of the first three colleges founded in Oxford. William, Archdeacon of Durham, died in 1249 leaving a legacy for the University to set up a house or college for ten Masters; this small community came into being and lived in successive halls until buildings were put up on the present site in the 1330s. The college was far from affluent and began to prosper only after the Reformation; in the 17th century several benefactions enabled Univ to undertake a thorough rebuilding that lasted, not without interruptions, for some thirty years from the 1630s onwards. (*See Merton and Balliol*)

The Front Quad, entered from The High, was begun in 1634; the statue on the street front of the gatehouse is of Queen Anne and on the inner front, facing the quad, there is a rare statue of the seldom-commemorated James II. The south range of the quad, opposite the gatehouse, is made up of the chapel and the hall, placed in line as in many other colleges. The hall, built in 1657 was remodelled in 1802, and extended westwards in 1904; the hammer-beam roof has survived the restorations and is largely original.

The chapel, completed and consecrated in 1666, was remodelled in 1862 when the ornamental stone-work, the east window and the roof were restored. The woodwork, including the screen, the stalls, and the panelling, is largely original 17th-century; there are, moreover, seven stained-glass windows of 1641 by Abraham van Linge, considered to be the best examples of this remarkable artist's work.

To the east of the Front Quad is the Radcliffe Quad; it was begun in 1716 with a bequest from Dr John Radcliffe, one of Oxford's most generous benefactors, who was a Univ man. This quad faithfully continues the design of the Front Quad of the previous century, which gives the buildings an unusual consistency of style. On the quad side of the gate-tower is a fine statue of Dr Radcliffe made by Francis Bird in 1717; on the street side one of Queen Mary II balances that of Queen Anne over the main gate. The gate from The High into the Radcliffe Quad has fine fan-vaulting. From the quad there is a gate into Logic Lane, now part of the college; on the near side of the lane, adjoining the quad, is the Master's Lodging, 1879; across the lane is the modern Goodhart Building of 1962; and at the High Street end, with a bridge over the lane, the Durham Building of 1903.

Fan vaulting in Radcliffe Quad, Univ

The view into Radcliffe Quad

Back in the Front Quad, a passage in the north-west corner leads to the Shelley Memorial. The poet was an undergraduate at Univ but was 'sent down' (expelled) in 1811 for writing and disseminating a pamphlet in support of atheism. After he was drowned in Italy in 1822 and buried in the Protestant Cemetery in Rome, his family commissioned a monument by Edward Onslow Ford. The Rome cemetery authorities would not allow it, but Univ accepted it and had this mausoleum built for it in 1894. The monument is judged to be an outstanding example of Victorian Romantic; some observers think the sculpture is not seen to best advantage in this rather gloomy setting; others that it is best relegated where it is.

The development of Univ to the west, beyond the Shelley Memorial, includes the New Buildings of 1842 by Charles Barry (famous for the Houses of Parliament) with a Victorian Gothic front on The High, and other 19th and 20th-century buildings approachable from Kybald Street and Magpie Lane.

From Univ it is a matter of crossing The High to reach The Queen's College. Its gateway, exactly opposite Logic Lane, is surmounted by a statue of Queen Caroline under a classical dome – a prominent feature of The High. From the college steps there are perspective views up and down the street in which its interesting curve may be appreciated.

The Queen's College, High Street. Founded 1341 by Robert de Eglesfield as The Provost and Scholars of the Queen's College in the University of Oxford.

Queen's is sixth in seniority, after Oriel and before New College. Eglesfield was a Cumberland man, who was chaplain to the consort of Edward III, Queen Philippa, under whose patronage the foundation was made, principally for Cumberland and Westmorland scholars; she was an

Front Quad, Queen's College

effective patron and herself gave revenues to the college as well as persuading the King to contribute endowments; the royal connection also helped Eglesfield to obtain benefactions from his friends. He arranged for future consorts to be invited to extend their patronage to the college, and later benefactresses included Henrietta Maria (consort of Charles I), Caroline (George II) whose statue is above the main gate, and Charlotte (George III).

Eglesfield's statutes laid down his ambitious ideas for the college membership, which was to consist, in the first place, of a Provost and twelve scholars (Fellows) representing Christ and the Apostles, thirteen chaplains, and seventy-two 'poor boys'. Eglesfield required the Provost and the twelve scholars to be seated at dinner in the manner traditional in paintings of *The Last Supper*, with the Provost on a throne; their gowns were to be crimson to remind them of the blood of Christ. They were to be summoned to dinner by a trumpet-call. Other less solemn observances included a

Queen Caroline

Christmas dinner with a boar's head; Christmas was celebrated in college on the supposition that scholars would not be able to return home to Cumberland and Westmorland in the winter.

Despite the royal patronage, the first three centuries of the college's existence were penurious; income was seldom enough to maintain more than a few chaplains and 'poor boys'. Consequently there were vacant rooms in the college buildings and Queen's began to admit *commensales* as early as the latter part of the 14th century, long before the admission of paying commoners became general among the other colleges, and earlier than Balliol and Exeter began to accept *sojourners*.

Because of inadequate income in the early years the college could not rebuild the huddle of medieval houses that it inhabited along Queen's Lane. Originally there was no frontage on The High, and the college did not acquire its present classical appearance until the 18th century.

Queen's as it appears today is the outcome of good management by successive Provosts in the second half of the 17th century and of several generous benefactions. After 1672 the college was able to start rebuilding and in 1692–5 to put up the most magnificent library of its time in Oxford. At the beginning of the 18th century William Lancaster, Provost 1704–17, launched an ambitious plan that did away with all the medieval hovels and replaced them with a consistent classical design for the whole college, attributed principally to Nicholas Hawksmoor. The most munificent, and timely, benefactor was Sir Joseph Williamson, 1633–1701, a 'poor boy' from Cockermouth, who became a Fellow in 1657, then entered Parliament, and by 1672 had become rich enough to give the college £1700 to put up the building bearing his name in the north-east corner of the college site. He was knighted in 1674 and in the same year became Secretary of State – a highly influential office for which he paid his predecessor £6000, later receiving the same amount from his successor. During the five years that he held this office he made good use of many opportunities of acquiring money, and he became extremely rich. He left Queen's a legacy of £6000 and his valuable collection of books. Williamson's death in 1701 coincided conveniently with the ambitious building plans of Provost Lancaster – marking a turning point in the college's architectural development.

The north range of the Front Quad, facing the gateway, contains the hall on the left of the central doorway and the chapel on the right. The hall, 1715, is magnificently baroque.

The chapel, consecrated in 1719, contains a lectern and stained glass surviving from the older chapel; eight of the windows are of 1636 and unmistakably by Abraham van Linge. The painting in the ceiling of the apse is an *Ascension* by James Thornhill.

The North Quad, which was built before the Front Quad, is severely classical; the west range, on the left, consists of the library, opened in 1695, attributed to Dean Henry Aldrich of Christ Church. Beyond the library, to the west, is a walled lane leading to Nunn's Garden and a group of buildings that include the old college brewery and Drawda Hall, an 18th-century house facing The High, named after the medieval scholar William of Drogheda who lived here.

Outside the original site of the college, on the other side of the lane, the Queen's Lane Quad was contrived in 1969–70 by adapting four old houses with fronts on The High and adding two modest blocks in the space backing onto St Edmund Hall. Queen's also owns the Florey Building (1971) in St Clement's on the far bank of the Cherwell, still one of Oxford's most controversial edifices.

Facing Queen's across the lane, a few yards up from The High, is the modest entrance to St Edmund Hall, which despite its name has full college status.

View over Queen's College into central Oxford

St Edmund Hall, Queen's Lane. Founded 12th-13th century; college status 1957.

Front Quad St Edmund Hall

This is the sole survivor of the numerous medieval halls that originally housed the scholars; its existence on this site dates from before 1270, when it was owned by Oseney Abbey. This would make it contemporary with Univ, Balliol and Merton; but it may be even older, since Edmund Rich of Abingdon is believed to have lived and taught on this site in the 1190s. He was a friend of Robert Grosseteste, was Archbishop of Canterbury 1233–40, and was canonized in 1248.

At the dissolution of Oseney Abbey in 1539 St Edmund Hall was left in a precarious position but was not dissolved. In 1557 it was bought by Queen's College and run as a subsidiary; it was ruled by a Principal and Vice-Principal, usually Fellows of Queen's, but it had no Fellows of its own; a small body of tutors was maintained to teach a fluctuating number of students.

The Hall continued as a semi-independent protectorate of Queen's up to the end of the 19th century, growing in academic status under several enlightened Principals, but it remained small and modest. From the beginning of the 20th century 'Teddy Hall' increased its autonomy by stages until in 1957 it acquired full college status, though its old name was not changed. It is now among the larger colleges, numerically, and has had to find ways of expanding its physical capacity beyond its original limited premises.

The front quad is virtually the only quad; it is small and informal with more the appearance of a garden or courtyard, and it even has a well-head; the buildings are of all ages, from the 16th century to the 20th. On the opposite side of the quad, facing the entrance from the lane, is the west front of the chapel of 1680; it has the ante-chapel below and a library above. There is a good contemporary screen, and some admirable stained glass by Edward Burne-Jones and William Morris, in whose workshops it was made. There is an altar painting of Christ at Emmaus, by Ceri Richards, 1958

A passage to the right of the chapel leads to the 1970 buildings, another example of the ingenious adaptation of old houses in The High and the addition of modern blocks in confined spaces.

Back in the front quad, a doorway in the north range leads to the 12th-century former church of St Peter-in-the-East, now the college library; only the crypt, of about 1100, is normally open to visitors. There was a Saxon church on this site from the 10th century or earlier.

To the right out of Teddy Hall, Queen's Lane runs north for a few yards and then turns westwards with Queen's library and Provost's Lodgings on the left and parts of New College on the right. Under an archway it joins New College Lane which leads to the Bridge of Sighs and so to The Broad again.

ITINERARY II

At the eastern end of The Broad, a little beyond Blackwell's, is the intersection of (anti-clockwise) Catte Street, Holywell Street, and Parks Road; the buildings on the four corners (also anti-clockwise) are: the Clarendon Building, already observed in Itinerary I; the 19th-century former Indian Institute, now the home of the History Faculty library; 'The King's Arms', a large and popular pub of 1607 but subsequently rebuilt and adapted upstairs by Wadham College; and fourth, the *New Bodleian Library*, in reality an extension with underground communication, designed by Sir Giles Gilbert Scott and built in 1937–40 but not opened until 1945. When it was completed the New Library was considered the ugliest building in Oxford, but in the intervening years other designs have overtaken it for this distinction.

This corner is the beginning of Parks Road; about a hundred yards along it, on the right, is Wadham College, its symmetrical front standing back from the road.

Wadham College, Parks Road. Founded 1610 by Nicholas and Dorothy Wadham, under the designation The Warden, Fellows and Scholars of Wadham College in the University of Oxford of the Foundation of Nicholas Wadham, Esquire, and Dorothy his wife.

Nicholas Wadham and his wife Dorothy, of Merifield in Somerset, were very rich gentry without children. Nicholas died in 1609 before any building had been begun, and it was Dorothy who carried out his intentions, adding a substantial contribution of her own. She was clearly a forceful personality; already in her seventies when Nicholas died. She bought the site of the Austin Friary in Parks Road, vacant since the Dissolution; she engaged a Merifield stone-mason-architect, William Arnold, who brought his own team of craftsmen to Oxford. She never herself came to Oxford but directed the whole operation from home by means of instructions to Arnold. Astonishingly, the college was built in three years, 1610–13, and the Warden and Fellows began to move in soon afterwards. Dorothy drew up the college statutes and appointed all the members of the college, including the servants, and continued to do so until she died in her eighties. She was the daughter of Sir William Petre (*see Exeter College*).

The college was disrupted by the Civil War, but the Warden appointed by the Parliamentarians, John Wilkins, was a serious academic and he attracted as Fellows several eminent scientists, including Christopher Wren. Wilkins and his Wadham colleagues, with other scientists from Cambridge, founded The Royal Society in 1662

Architecturally Wadham is unlike most Oxford colleges in having been designed and built under one man, and in having suffered no modifications, modernizations or Victorianizations in its fabric. The Front Quad has a four-tier frontispiece, exactly contemporary with those at Merton (Fellows' Quad) and in the Old Schools Quad. Here the statues are of King James I and of Nicholas and Dorothy Wadham.

The chapel is T-shaped in the Oxford tradition and is notable for its admirable screen of 1613, and other 17th-century woodwork. The organ case, the reredos and the stone panelling round the altar are 19th-century. The east window is dated 1622 and is by Bernard van Linge (Abraham's brother); the side windows in the choir are also of the 17th century.

Opposite, Wadham College Garden and the Bowra Building

Frontispiece, James I and founders

The hall is remarkable for its great size, for its original hammer-beam roof, and for another fine contemporary screen. To the east of the hall is the Cloister Quad formed by the chapel (to the north) and the kitchen, and open to the east looking into a corner of the gardens; under the trees is John Doubleday's bronze bust of Sir Maurice Bowra, Warden 1938–70, under whose long and inspiring reign Wadham achieved further eminence.

There have been three modern extension programmes at Wadham, largely centred on the Back Quad (south of the main buildings). First, in 1951–4, the New Building along the east side of the quad; then in 1971–2 the development of the 'King's Arms' and the other houses in Holywell Street, including Blackwell's Music Shop; and more recently the block housing the new library.

From the Front Quad, via the chapel doorway, it is worth going into the Fellows' Garden with its magnificent trees.

Across Parks Road, facing Wadham's gatehouse, is a fine wrought-iron screen of 1713, through which there is a view of the spacious garden and distant buildings of Trinity College, where this itinerary ends. Meanwhile Parks Road may be followed northwards (to the right out of Wadham) past a pair of 17th-century cottages on the right and on the left a high wall concealing the garden of St John's College and its new Garden Quad building.

View from the north, over the Science Area.

The Science Area. Next, on the right, is the junction of South Parks Road, which marks the beginning of the Science Area. The first building on the north side of the road, on the corner, is *The Radcliffe Science Library* containing the scientific books bequeathed to the University by Dr John Radcliffe, for which the Camera was originally built. The north side of South Parks Road, for the rest of its length, is occupied by laboratories and lecture rooms of the science faculties – and there are others northwards along Parks Road. These buildings are less important for their architecture than for the achievements of scientists working in them. It was in the Pathology Department, for instance, that in the late 1930s and early 40s Sir Howard (later Lord) Florey and his distinguished team developed the clinical application of penicillin, which had been discovered in 1928 by Sir Alexander Fleming.

On the south side of South Parks Road, a short distance from the corner, is *Rhodes House* (1929), identifiable by its neo-classical portico projecting from a shallow-domed rotunda surmounted by a bronze Zimbabwe bird – a modern copy of a prehistoric original. Cecil Rhodes: his most important benefaction to Oxford was the founding of the Rhodes Scholarships, intended principally to bring graduates from the English-speaking world, and also from Germany, to Oxford for three years' studies. The first Rhodes Scholars came in 1903; the number of them in Oxford in any year is normally over seventy, and they now include women. Rhodes House is the academic, social and administrative centre of the system, and it houses the relevant sections of the Bodleian Library. (*see also Oriel College*).

Parks Road continues northwards to the older science area, the centre-piece of which is The University Museum, the first and still the most impressive of science buildings in Oxford.

Rhodes House from Wadham College Garden

The University Museum (1860). This imposing Victorian Gothic structure was the outcome of efforts by Sir Henry Acland, Regius Professor of Medicine, and John Ruskin to set up a museum where everything then known in natural history could be concentrated in one place, together with the teaching of the sciences. Behind the eminently civic front is a vast hall with a steeply pitched glass roof supported by cast iron gothic arches (described by Acland as 'railway materials'), all of admirable design and superb workmanship. It was at the newly built University Museum that in 1860 the British Association staged the famous debate on evolution in which Samuel Wilberforce, Bishop of Oxford, was roundly defeated in argument with the

Acland's ' Railway Materials'

brilliant Thomas Huxley, friend and supporter of Charles Darwin.[4] (*see also Botanic Garden*).

The Pitt Rivers Museum of Ethnology, built close to the University Museum in 1885–6 to house the huge collection of anthropological exhibits amassed over many years by Lieut-General Augustus Henry Lane Fox Pitt Rivers (1827–1900); it is one of the world's major ethnological museums and is also a teaching institution in the University Department of Ethnology and Prehistory. There is an extension at No 60 Banbury Road.

To the north of the University Museum and some adjacent science buildings lie the *University Parks*, a large open area of grass and trees – many of them exotic – bordered on the east by the River Cherwell, and containing the University Cricket Ground. In the south-east corner of the Parks is the point where the river divides to form the elongated island walk known as Mesopotamia. A little farther up-stream the river is spanned by Rainbow Bridge, a footbridge leading to a riverside path on the far bank that goes northwards to Wolfson College and 'The Victoria Arms', Marston.

Facing the Museum across Parks Road is Keble College, architecturally as challenging today as when it was built.

Keble College, Parks Road. Founded 1868 by the Oxford Movement, with public subscription.

Keble College was founded by the Tractarians, leaders of the Oxford Movement, partly as an act of Christian faith, partly as a memorial to John Keble, who died in 1866, and partly in response to the perceived need to provide opportunities at Oxford for poor students, severely restricted since the abolition of servitors in the 1854 reforms. There was no powerful bene-factor and no government help. However, in 1866, after Keble's death, the Archbishop of

Canterbury launched an appeal for public subscriptions, which was extraordinarily successful. After only two years the college could be founded, and building was begun.

The founders chose as architect William Butterfield, himself a supporter of the Oxford Movement. Keble College is thought to be not only his most ambitious but also his most successful creation; though after more than a century the buildings are as controversial as ever. It is generally conceded that the proportions are noble and the placing of the component buildings is masterly, especially as seen from the central Liddon Quad with its attractive sunken lawn. There is less agreement over Butterfield's use of polychrome bricks in dazzling patterns in a city where stone predominates. Ruskin, whose ideals were embodied in the University Museum, abandoned his habit of taking a daily walk in the Parks because he could not tolerate what he saw of the chapel as it was being built. Other observers have found it stimulating and cheerful;

'It must be the most single-minded building in England.... It rings through the architectural timidities of Oxford like a fanfare – or more accurately, perhaps, a fire-bell. A contemporary critic has described the chapel as looking like a dinosaur in a Fair Isle sweater. Well, yes and no. The thick skin, the sense of weight, the woven pattern of the walls, the hint of the comic that always surrounds any human obsession is all encapsulated in this witty phrase; but it is not, in my view, the truth, which is that the chapel is indeed a masterpiece.' (Sir Hugh Casson).

In accordance with the Tractarians' eucharistic concepts, the seating in the chapel is forward-facing, as in a parish church, and not in the collegiate pattern. There is a small side chapel

Keble and Oxford

(not by Butterfield) containing the original first version of William Holman Hunt's painting *The Light of the World*.

Keble College's contribution to modern architecture consists of a block running the length of Blackhall Road, at the back of the college site. This building, all in yellowish brick, out of harmony with Butterfield, presents a blank face to the street but its inner front is mainly glass. The new 'Arco' building in extremely red brick was put up on the Keble Road front in 1995; it too is not strikingly in harmony with the older buildings.

The original scheme to provide opportunities for indigent young men 'desirous of entering the Christian Ministry' would have made Keble an Anglican theological college, but the first Warden, Edward Talbot, opened the college to all comers, not only to ordinands. Communion in the Anglican Church, at first an essential condition for all members of the college, was waived, for undergraduates in 1930, for Fellows in 1952, and for the Warden in 1969.

A short way to the left out of Keble's main gate leads to the junction of Parks Road with Keble Road, which latter runs along the north side of the college buildings. and joins the Banbury Road opposite *St Giles' Church*.

This church may also be reached at the end of a detour embracing several important establishments in North Oxford. This more ambitious itinerary continues up Parks Road to its end, and there branches right into Norham Gardens.

Keble College Chapel from the Parks

Lady Margaret Hall (L.M.H) Norham Gardens. Founded in 1878 by Dame Elizabeth Wordsworth.

This was the first college specifically intended for the higher education of women members of the Church of England: it was set up by the determination of Elizabeth Wordsworth with the support of the Association for the Education of Women in Oxford, and was named after Lady Margaret Beaufort, Countess of Richmond, the mother of Henry VII and a patron of learning. L.M.H achieved full college status in 1959 but did not change its name. In 1979 the college opened its doors to men and appointed a man as Principal.

The buildings at L.M.H are of various dates in the 19th and 20th centuries and are by several architects; but they combine to form a harmonious neo-Georgian group, much enhanced by its superb position beside the River Cherwell.

A short distance to the north are Bardwell Road, where *The Dragon School* has its principal building, and Chadlington Road, from which a lane leads to *The Cherwell Boat House*, where there are punts for hire, and a restaurant. Immediately north of this is Wolfson College.

Wolfson College, Linton Road. Founded at Iffley in 1965 by the University; college status was achieved in 1981.

The college was originally set up in Iffley as a small graduate community. Grants from the

Wolfson College

Wolfson and the Ford Foundations, and the University's gift of the magnificent site on the River Cherwell, resulted in a much larger establishment for resident graduates, including their families, from all over the world.

The architects were Powell and Moya whose buildings here have an attractive riverside setting with a private punt-harbour and a footbridge over the Cherwell.

From Wolfson College westwards Linton Road connects with the Banbury Road; this much-used highway runs north to Summertown, a self-contained suburb dating from the 19th century and the home of *St Edward's* and other schools, as also of the local station of the BBC, and of the headquarters of *Oxfam*.

This itinerary, however, turns south in the Banbury Road until it reaches St Margaret's Road running west. Near the corner is the main entrance of St Hugh's College.

St Hugh's College, St Margaret's Road. Founded 1886 by Dame Elizabeth Wordsworth, her second foundation intended as a simpler, more economical alternative to L.M.H.

The new venture began modestly in a private house in Norham Gardens, but it was highly successful and grew rapidly. By 1916 St Hugh's had acquired its present site, and the first buildings in a dignified neo-Georgian style were completed. Since then the College's residential capacity on this site has been greatly enlarged, and its buildings occupy the whole of the south side of St Margaret's Road as far as its junction with the Woodstock Road. St Hugh's, along

St. Hugh's College

with the other women's colleges achieved full college status in 1959 and welcomes men as well as women. One of the most notable features of St Hugh's is its garden, or complex of gardens, created by Miss Annie Rogers, a distinguished classicist and an admirer of the celebrated gardener Miss Gertrude Jekyll.

Continuing southwards along the Banbury Road leads on the east side to the elegant enclave of *Park Town*, a haven of 1850s houses with virtually no road traffic since there is no through road. On the west side of the Banbury Road is North Parade Avenue, a miniature high street with an agreeable variety of shops and restaurants. It leads into Church Walk, a pedestrian path along the south side of the massive, and now redundant, Church of SS. Philip and James on the Woodstock Road. A left turn at this point leads past the buildings of St Antony's College and to its principal entrance.

St Antony's College, Woodstock Road. Founded in 1948 by the University with the help of a substantial donation from a French businessman M. Antonin Besse.

The foundation was able to acquire the buildings of a former Anglican convent built in 1868 in gloomy Victorian Gothic. In 1970 a new modern building was put up at a slight distance to the north, and some neighbouring Victorian houses have since been acquired.

St Antony's had the status of a New Foundation from 1950 until 1965, when it became fully collegiate. It is a graduate college with special emphasis on studies related to other regions of the world, and it receives visiting Fellows and graduate students from many other countries.

St Antony's site is bordered on the south side by Bevington Road, on the other side of which is the area occupied by St Anne's College between the Banbury and Woodstock Roads.

St. Anne's College

St Anne's College, Woodstock Road. Founded 1879 by the Association for the Education of Women in Oxford as *The Society of Home Students*.

The Society was set up to provide an academic vehicle for young women living in Oxford – dons' daughters for example – who wanted a university education. The Society began its existence in the North Oxford private house of the first Principal, Mrs Bertha Johnson. By the 1920s the number of undergraduates was increasing rapidly and was no longer confined to Oxford residents; the 1930s saw the beginning of many benefactions resulting in the ownership of the present large site.

The Society became St Anne's College by incorporation in 1952, and acquired full college status in 1959; in 1976 the statutes were changed to admit men, who now account for about half the membership.

Across the Woodstock Road from St Anne's is the modest, almost rural, gateway and first quad of Green College partly concealed by a high wall.

The Radcliffe Observatory, Green College

Green College and Radcliffe Observatory, Woodstock Road. Founded in 1979 by the University and a group of benefactors led by Dr Cecil Green of Texas Instruments Inc.

The Observatory became in 1977 the nucleus of Green College, founded as a graduate college for clinical medical students and others working in related disciplines. The entrance in Woodstock Road leads into Lankester Quad, named after the architect, and into the admirable gardens.

The Observatory was another of Dr John Radcliffe's benefactions to the University, carried out by his trustees. The buildings, with the central 'Tower of Winds', were begun in 1772 under Henry Keene and completed by James Wyatt in 1794; the original inspiration is said to be the Tower of Winds in Athens, of the 1st century BC. *Pevsner* considers it to be 'architecturally the finest observatory of Europe'. It ceased to be an observatory in 1935, and the instruments were transferred to the Museum of the History of Science in the Old Ashmolean Building.

The Radcliffe Infirmary. Virtually adjoining Green College is the Radcliffe Infirmary, one of the several benefactions made by the trustees of Dr John Radcliffe. The original plain Georgian building of 1770, looking onto a garden forecourt with a fountain copied from Bernini's *Triton*, is now surrounded by ugly accretions built over two centuries to accommodate the Infirmary's ever-increasing activities. It began as a university institution and soon gained academic eminence, which increased both with the development of clinical laboratory research and with its teaching role, especially under Professor Henry Acland in the years 1847–79 and Professor William Osler in 1905–19. In 1936 the Infirmary received from Lord Nuffield a large benefaction that led to the creation of eight professorships, making it one of Britain's principal medical teaching institutions. The first intravenous injection of penicillin was given to a patient in the Infirmary by Dr Charles Fletcher in 1941. Most of the clinical activities are now at the John Radcliffe Hospital in Headington and at the Churchill and Nuffield Hospitals, also in Headington. Adjoining the Infirmary is Somerville College.

Somerville College, Woodstock Road. Founded 1878 by the Association for the Education of Women in Oxford.

Somerville, like LMH, was brought into being by the Association for the Education of Women in Oxford but was established as non-denominational (whereas LMH was specifically for Anglicans). The foundation was named after Mary Somerville (1780–1872), a distinguished scientist and promotor of women's education and suffrage. The college began its life in Walton House on the present site, subsequently acquiring a large area of land between Walton Street and Woodstock Road and southwards to Little Clarendon Street. Several architects have worked at Somerville over the century and the various buildings are in diverse styles, not helped by having had to be fitted round the Victorian Gothic of *St Aloysius' Church*. Somerville achieved full college status at the same time as the other women's colleges in 1959.

St Aloysius (1875) was designed by J. A. Hansom, who also designed the Hansom cab. The incumbent priest in 1878–9 was Gerard Manley Hopkins.

The annual St Giles' fair

St Giles. The parish church of St Giles stands on a narrow site between the Woodstock and Banbury Roads; the building dates from the 1130s, but only a few traces of Norman masonry have survived the extensive restorations of the 19th century. To the south of the church, where the War Memorial stands, the two roads converge to become the wide tree-lined avenue known simply as St Giles' or 'The Giler'.

Pevsner considers that the avenue contains 'the best sequence of 18th-century houses,' especially on the east side: Queen Elizabeth House, St Giles' House ('the best house of its date in Oxford'), belonging to St John's College, Middleton Hall, and the greater part of St John's College itself. On the west side is *St Benet's Hall*, a Benedictine foundation of 1899 to enable members of Ampleforth Abbey to matriculate at Oxford, after their exclusion for some four centuries after the Dissolution..

Next on the west side after Somerville College is the entrance to *Little Clarendon Street*, with pedestrian access to Wellington Square. In this conglomeration of large 19th-century houses and modern concrete blocks are the offices of several administrative departments of the University, as well as shops and restaurants. On the corner of Wellington Square and St John Street stands the domestic-looking building known as *Rewley House*.

Kellogg College – Rewley House. Wellington Square. The idea of making university-class education available to the people in general was first expressed in 1850, but adult external studies did not begin until 1878. From 1885 the number of pupils increased rapidly and was further promoted by the institution of residential summer schools; this led to the setting up of the Workers' Educational Association (WEA). These activities were eventually co-ordinated at Rewley House under the Delegacy for Extra-Mural Studies and later developed with grants from the Kellogg Foundation for the enlargement of living quarters at Rewley House, which is now the home of the Department for Continuing Education and a collegiate residential institution. In 1990 Kellogg College became the thirty-sixth college federated with the University.

Rewley House

Continuing southwards along St John Street leads to Pusey Street on the left, which in turn leads back to St Giles. In Pusey Street is *Regent's Park College*, a Baptist theological college founded in London in 1810 and moved to Oxford in 1940. Its status is that of a Permanent Private Hall, which means that its students may matriculate and graduate, but it is not fully independent.

'The Eagle and Child', 1650. A few yards north of Pusey Street there is in St Giles an attractive row of old houses including a small pub 'The Eagle and Child' or familiarly 'The Bird and Baby'. It was the regular meeting-place of C. S. Lewis, Charles Williams, Nevill Coghill, J. R. R. Tolkien, and others, who formed the literary group known as 'The Inklings'. On the south face of the inn-sign the baby is dangling from the eagle's talons, but on the north face he has somehow mounted the eagle's back and is riding pretty.

St Cross College, Pusey House, St Giles. Founded 1966 by the University to provide a college life for non-collegiate lecturers and graduate students. It began in an old school house near St Cross Church, then in 1981 obtained the lease of part of Pusey House which it shares with the library of the Theology Faculty.

Blackfriars Priory, St Giles. A Dominican house built in 1921–29 when the Order returned to Oxford after an absence, since the Dissolution, of almost four centuries. The buildings are described by *Pevsner* as 'somewhat tired Gothic', but are skilfully fitted into a limited site.

St Giles' Fair. Since the 18th century what was a simple parish wake has developed into an annual event in early September known as *St Giles' Fair*. This occupies the whole of the avenue for two days with a huge concentration of stalls, booths, fortune-tellers, and countless fair-ground machines ranging from classical merry-go-rounds to much more alarming devices. John Betjeman believed, in 1937, that it was 'about the biggest fair in England.'

This itinerary now crosses St Giles to the east side, beckoned by the principal gateway of St John's College.

St John's College, St Giles. Founded 1555 by Sir Thomas White as The President and Scholars of Saint John Baptist College in the University of Oxford.

St John's was founded after the Reformation but in the reign of Mary Tudor, by a Roman Catholic layman who was anxious that scholars should be taught to combat the heresies of Protestantism. Sir Thomas White (1492–1567), a rich member of the Merchant Taylors' Company and Alderman of the City of London, in 1555 acquired the then new – and even unfinished – buildings of St Bernard's College, a Cistercian monastic house of 1437 that had been dissolved in 1539. He was able to set up his college immediately; his statutes of 1558 call for the inclusion of scholars of his own kin and from the Merchant Taylors' School, founded about the same time with his participation.

Thanks to White's ample endowments, St John's was able to acquire Walton and Norham Manors, which include most of today's suburb of North Oxford; he thus laid the foundations of the college's important role as a landowner in Oxford, which has continued.

The notable achievements of the 16th century were, however, surpassed by the abundant benefactions of the college's most eminent member in the 17th century. William Laud became a Fellow in 1589, then President in 1611, and Chancellor of the University in 1629. He was also Bishop of Bath and Wells in 1626, and of London in 1682; personal adviser and confidant of Charles I from about 1625 to 1629, and Archbishop of Canterbury in 1633. Laud was powerful and he was able to increase both the revenues and the buildings of St John's. He was succeeded as President of the college by William Juxon, who came to St John's from Merchant Taylors' School in 1598. He became President in 1621 and in 1627 Vice-Chancellor of the University – an office created by Laud. Juxon left the presidency of St John's in 1633 to become

Garden front of Canterbury Quad, St John's

St John's, Canterbury Quad

Bishop of London; he lost his see under the Parliamentarians, but was made Archbishop of Canterbury at the Restoration; he was succeeded as President by Richard Baylie, who built the Baylie Chapel.

The west front of the college, with the gatehouse tower on St Giles is part of the old St Bernard's buildings. The statue above the gate, representing St John the Baptist, began its existence as a figure of St Bernard; it is now accompanied by Archbishop Chichele, founder of St Bernard's, and Sir Thomas White. Inside the Front Quad, is another statue of St John the Baptist, by Eric Gill, put up in 1936.

Most of the Front Quad is St Bernard's, except for the crenellations added in the 17th-century and the sash windows that replaced casements in the 18th; the east range opposite the gate, lacked its roof at the Dissolution but was completed by Sir Thomas White as the college library. The north range, on the left, contains the chapel and the hall, aligned in the usual way. The chapel is Cistercian from 1530, but it has been much changed in subsequent centuries, and is of slight architectural interest, except perhaps for the adjoining Baylie Chapel of 1662, with its fine plaster fan-vault and the tombs of Sir Thomas White and Archbishops Laud and Juxon.

The hall, the other half of the north range, is where the kitchen of St Bernard's had been, but the interior is largely of the 18th century. The buttery, however, with its vaulted cellar is original 15th-century.

Beyond the chapel and hall is the North Quad: on the left, Cook's Building (1643, one of Laud's gifts) followed northwards by the New Building of 1880 and other additions of different dates, including on the right the earliest example (1960) of a college building that can be called 'modern' in the sense that it owes nothing to earlier architectural fashions; it is known as 'The Beehive' because of its hexagonal modules. Farther north, beyond the quad, is the Sir Thomas White Building of 1977 facing south over a garden and backing onto Lamb & Flag Alley, uncompromisingly modern.

Back to the Front Quad: through the fan-vaulted passage-way in the east range, is Canterbury Quad. This was William Laud's greatest gift to his college, completed in 1636 three years after he became Archbishop of Canterbury. It is, as *Pevsner* remarks, a 'princely job' and 'by far the most impressive building of its date in Oxford'. The east and the west ranges are exuberantly ornamented with grand portals, frontispieces and arcades, the east with a bronze statue of Charles I and the west with one of Henrietta Maria, both by Hubert Lesueur. The design of this quad had to accommodate the already existing west and south ranges – not closely related to each other – which it did by repeating the details in the new buildings. *Pevsner* believes the designer was either Nicholas Stone of Oxford or Adam Browne, who worked at Lambeth Palace.

The portal in the east range leads into the superb garden affording a view of the west front – the outer face – of Canterbury Quad, a long, dignified, serene building of great quality. The far wall of the garden, as already noted, runs along Parks Road. Where this wall reaches the northern boundary of the site the college has put up an ambitious building, the Garden Quad, completed in 1996. It is in St John's tradition of bold innovation as exemplified in the Beehive and the Sir Thomas White Building, but in style it owes nothing to these. There remains, to the south of Canterbury Quad, the Holmes Building, dating from 1794, pleasant but not extraordinary, and Dolphin Quad on an old inn site reached from the south west corner of Front Quad.

Martyrs' Memorial. To the left out of St John's – that is southwards – St Giles leads to the Martyrs' Memorial, built in 1843 by public subscription nearly three centuries after the martyrdom; the design is by George Gilbert Scott and is based on the Eleanor Cross of the 1290s at Waltham, considered the best preserved of the three surviving from the twelve built in 1291–4 by Edward I to mark the resting places of the funeral procession of his Queen Eleanor, who had died at Nottingham and was taken to be buried at Westminster Abbey. This cross in Oxford commemorates the burning for heresy of three Protestant churchmen, Bishops Nicholas Ridley and Hugh Latimer, and Archbishop Thomas Cranmer in 1555–6. (*See Introduction, Bloody Mary*)

Immediately to the south of the memorial is the church of *St Mary Magdalen*; the building incorporates some components of the 14th century, but it was heavily restored in the 19th. The short street along the east side of the church leads into Broad Street, where the principal front of Balliol College begins. A few yards along, in the centre of the carriageway, a cross of granite setts let into the surface is alleged to mark the spot where the Protestant Martyrs were burned at the stake, as is explained in an inscribed stone plaque on the wall of the college. A few yards farther is the main gate of Balliol.

St. John's College

Balliol College, Broad Street. Founded 1263 by John de Balliol (or Bailleul) and Princess Dervorguilla as The Master and Scholars of Balliol College in the University of Oxford.

This is one of the three oldest foundations, and was the first to occupy a permanent site of its

Balliol, the Broad Street Front

own, which it did in the year of its founding. John de Balliol of Barnard Castle, County Durham, was an arrogant baron married to the Scottish Princess Dervorguilla. About 1255 he quarrelled with the Bishop of Durham over the ownership of certain lands; the Bishop, with the King behind him, was the more powerful and Balliol lost the argument; the Bishop had him scourged in public, and imposed a further penance that he should set up in Oxford a house for sixteen poor scholars and maintain them at his own expense. By 1260 Balliol had found or built a tenement outside the city wall beyond the ditch, roughly where the Master's Lodging now stands; the community was probably fully established by 1263. Balliol died in 1269 and Dervorguilla later completed his undertaking by conferring endowments and statutes on the house.

The college survived the brief mastership of the 'heretical' John Wycliffe (in 1360–I) but continued only precariously under Dervorguilla's restrictive statutes, until Bishop Richard Fox (founder of Corpus Christi) drew up new, workable, statutes in 1507. In the 15th century the college, still obscure and far from rich, had begun to accept *sojourners*; these were paying lodgers similar to *commensales* at Queen's.

Balliol continued to be academically undistinguished and financially insecure up to the end of the 18th-century; in the 19th, however, four Masters – John Parsons, Richard Jenkyns, Robert Scott (of the Greek lexicon with Liddell of Christ Church) and Benjamin Jowett – who together spanned the century, changed the policy of the college in the election of scholars and Fellows and so achieved the academic excellence that was to ensure the college's eminence and its reputation for 'effortless superiority'.

Architecturally Balliol is unremarkable. The Broad Street front, including the Master's Lodging, is 19th-century 'Balmoral Gothic'. The Fisher building on the corner is a century older but equally uninspired. Northwards from the corner, back up St Giles, the other long front is a succession of 19th and early 20th-century buildings of little architectural distinction.

The Front Quad is small and contains the only ancient buildings on the site; opposite the main gate, to the left of the narrow passage, is the old library, of the 15th century still in use.

At right angles to it, making the west range, is the former hall, now the main library, also of the 15th century; both these buildings were remodelled in the 1790s.

The Front Quad also contains the chapel, 1856–7 by William Butterfield,(*see Keble*) replacing an earlier building of 1529. The pulpit and the eagle lectern date from the 1630s; there are two windows of the same period by Abraham van Linge, and much of the other glass is older (1529–30). The silver-gilt altar-front was given in 1927.

A passageway in the north-west corner of the Front Quad leads to the Garden Quad – perhaps Balliol's most attractive feature – once known as The Grove. In the passageway are the old gates, which were in use from the 16th century or earlier, said to have been scorched by the fire in which the Protestant Bishops were martyred; these gates were thrown out during the 19th-century rebuilding, but were recovered by chance.

The Garden Quad is large, much more a garden than it is a quad, and it has fine trees. South, on the left, is the inner face of the Master's Lodgings; along the west side are the inner fronts of the buildings along St Giles, ending with two buildings of the 1960s; adjoining these is the hall, 1876, with a fine flight of steps. Inside, unusually, there is an organ, given by Jowett to encourage the use of the hall for music. To the right of the hall is another modern building. The enclosure on the east side of the quad is the Fellows' Garden containing some ancient mulberry trees and an assembly of pieces of masonry facetiously known as 'Dervorguilla's Tomb'.

To the left out of Balliol's gate, within a few yards is Trinity College; the first view of it is through fine wrought-iron gates but the entrance is through the first of the cottages on The Broad.

Fellows' Garden and 'Dervorguilla's Tomb'

Entrance to the Garden Quad

Trinity College, Broad Street. Founded 1555 by Sir Thomas Pope as The President, Fellows and Scholars of the College of the Holy and Undivided Trinity in the University of Oxford.

Trinity stands on the site of the medieval Durham College, one of the monastic houses set up by the Benedictines, for their scholars from the north of England. After the Dissolution of the Monasteries in 1539 the college tried to subsist as a private hall, but it failed and was closed in 1544.

Sir Thomas Pope (1507–59), who had amassed a fortune in the service of Henry VIII, acquired the land and buildings of Durham College and in 1555 obtained from Mary Tudor a charter for the foundation of Trinity College. He was not, it seems, a fervent or a declared Roman Catholic, since he was Treasurer of the Court of Augmentations handling the revenues that accrued to the Crown from the dissolved monasteries. He was knighted by Henry VIII and was one of the King's financial executors.

Although Sir Thomas endowed his foundation generously, he seems to have had no special aim such as combating heresy or providing for his kin; the college progressed only slowly until 1599 when the energetic and eccentric Ralph Kettell became President. He made the college academically eminent and materially prosperous; and he built a new dining hall when the old one collapsed. Besides being energetic and efficient Kettell seems to have been a strict disciplinarian and also a man of great kindness. John Aubrey (*Brief Lives*) was a student at Trinity in the 1640s and describes Kettell as prying about the college and looking through keyholes to see if the scholars were at work; he disliked long hair, and sometimes carried in his muff a pair of

A doorway in Trinity

Trinity, the chapel

scissors with which he would chop the hair of those sitting on the outer side of the tables in hall. He was also very generous and would put gifts of money in at the windows of scholars whom he believed to be indigent. Aubrey also records that Kettell had observed 'the houses that had the smallest beer had the most drunkards, for it forced them to go into the town to comfort their stomachs, wherefore Dr Kettell always had in his college excellent beer, not better to be had in Oxon, so that we had the fewest drunkards in any house in Oxford.'

During the occupation of Oxford in the Civil War, Dr Kettell was much put out by the notoriously licentious behaviour of the Court ladies, and by the rudeness of the soldiers. Aubrey concludes that the life of 'the good old Doctor' was shortened by these disruptions.

Kettell's equally energetic grandson Ralph Bathurst was President 1664–1704; he continued what Kettell had begun and made Trinity a place both of architectural distinction and of intellectual eminence. Bathurst was a practising physician as well as an academic scientist; he was a friend of Christopher Wren, and he was one of the scientific group who with Wilkins of Wadham contributed to the foundation in 1662 of the Royal Society in London.

Inside the garden-like Front Quad, with the walls of Balliol on the left, the most prominent building is on the right: a long gabled and ornamented neo-Jacobean range of 1887 by Thomas G. Jackson virtually fills the east side of the quad. The detached building at the northern end is the President's Lodging. In the south-east corner of the quad, with its front on The Broad, is Kettell Hall, built in 1620 as an investment rather than as part of the college, but now fully integrated.

The central group of buildings, on the far side of the lawn, begins with the chapel, with the gatehouse attached to it (the main entrance was originally here), built under the impetus of President Bathurst and completed about 1692; the design is attributed to Dean Henry Aldrich of Christ Church but cannot be dissociated from Christopher Wren. The outstandingly fine wood-carving is thought to be by Grinling Gibbons. *Pevsner* considers the chapel to be 'one of the most perfect ensembles of the late 17th-century in the whole country', marred only by poor stained glass. The chapel forms the south range of Durham Quad, so called for being the site of the medieval college. The east range on the right is the only remaining 15th-century building, though its age is not apparent; it contains the old library with some 15th-century glass possibly transposed from the old chapel. The so-called cock-lofts were added in 1602 as rooms for commoners.

North of Durham Quad is the Garden Quad, which began as a detached building (1668), by Christopher Wren, but had the west range added in 1682; and the whole balance of the buildings was altered by the addition in 1802 of a third storey. The open east side of the quad looks out over the vast lawns towards the wrought-iron gates in Parks Road, facing Wadham.

Trinity has access westwards to St Giles through its 1948 Dolphin Gatehouse which separates St John's from Balliol. 'The Dolphin' was a medieval inn. To the east of the Front Quad is Trinity's modern extension: the Cumberbatch Quad, completed in 1968 and consisting of a group of varied buildings. Below this quad, by a remarkable feat of architectural engineering is Blackwell's *Norrington Room* said to be the largest book display in the world.

Opposite: Central Oxford from Trinity College Tower

ITINERARY III

Facing Blackwells bookshop across the Broad is the north face of Exeter College, which stretches from Turl Street to the Old Ashmolean. This Itenerary now goes into Turl Street (The Turl), where there are three colleges and the Covered Market.

Exeter College, Turl Street. Founded in 1314 by Walter de Stapledon, Bishop of Exeter, as the Rector and Scholars of Exeter College in the University of Oxford.

The college is the fourth oldest in Oxford, next after the disputed three; it was founded by Walter de Stapledon, for scholars from his diocese. The founder set up his community in 1312 in Hart Hall (*see Hertford College*) which he renamed Stapledon Hall; two years later he moved the scholars to St Stephen's Hall, which was later enlarged by the acquisition of adjoining buildings, and in 1405 the name Exeter College was adopted. Its endowments were far from large, however, and Bishop Stapledon's statutes were too restrictive to be workable; the college was in penury for most of the 15th century, but it survived by taking in *sojourners* (as Balliol did). One of these, William Petre (1505–1572), became a generous benefactor after he retired in 1566 from the remunerative public office of Secretary of State under Queen Elizabeth. He rewrote the statutes, endowed several fellowships, and bequeathed to the college his valuable library, which included the 14th-century illuminated Bohun Psalter. He was the father of Dorothy Wadham (*see Wadham College*).

The improvement in Exeter's fortunes and academic status begun by Sir William Petre was carried forward by the energetic John Prideaux, Rector of the college 1612–42 and Vice Chancellor 1619–24; he attracted benefactions and encouraged the building of the hall, of the adjoining range known as Peryam's Buildings overlooking the Fellows' Garden, and of an elegant chapel – which was demolished in 1854 to make room for George Gilbert Scott's creation.

Continuing prosperity in the 17th century enabled the college to build the Turl Street range in 1672 and 1703, including a new gatehouse and main entrance. The only surviving medieval building is Palmer's Tower, of 1432, on the east side of the quad facing the main gate; this was the first gatehouse, on a long-vanished lane, and it is now the Rector's Lodging. The Turl Street front was originally neo-classical in style, but it was gothicized in 1834 and purged of all classical details except the vaulting inside the gatehouse.

The hall is on the south side of the quad (on the right seen from the gatehouse). It dates from 1618 and retains, intact and unspoiled, its original delicately built collar-beam roof; it also has a fine Jacobean screen.

On the opposite side of the quad, facing the hall, is the chapel of 1860 by George Gilbert Scott, reliably said to be inspired by, if not actually copied from, the Abbot's Chapel at the Cistercian Abbey of Chaâlis, north of Paris, built about 1250. Exeter's version is too large in relation to its setting and is still the subject of divergent opinions. The neatest comment is Sir Hugh Casson's: 'If you like this sort of thing, this is the sort of thing you will like.' Inside the chapel, at the east end of the south wall hangs a tapestry, *The Adoration of the Magi*, by Edward

Opposite: Exeter College, Library and Fellows' Garden

Burne-Jones and William Morris, both members of the college. To the north of the chapel is Margary Quad with a gate on The Broad; the quad is formed by 19th and 20th-century buildings of no great architectural distinction.

On the east side of the main quad (facing the gatehouse) the doorway of Staircase V leads into the Fellows' Garden, small but attractive, with the college library and the Divinity School along one side and a good view of the Radcliffe Camera from the embankment at the far end. Facing Exeter across The Turl is Jesus College.

Jesus College, Turl Street. Founded in 1571 as The Principal, Fellows and Scholars of Jesus College within the City and University of Oxford, of Queen Elizabeth's foundation.

In fact the college was set up by Hugh Price, Treasurer of St David's Cathedral, Pembroke. He enjoyed Queen Elizabeth's patronage and her help in obtaining possession of the 13th-century White Hall and several adjacent houses on this same site. His foundation was intended primarily for Welsh scholars, and the college has retained strong Welsh connections to this day.

Price was already aged 76 when he made the foundation, and he died three years later before he could give the college its statutes. The first fifty years were penurious, but from 1621 there were three successive vigorous Principals who obtained approval of the statutes, attracted useful benefactions, and advanced the college both academically and architecturally; the last of the three, Leoline Jenkins, later became Secretary of State and acquired a substantial fortune, which he bequeathed to the college when he died in 1685; he was thereafter acknowledged as the second founder.

The front facing onto The Turl is almost the only Elizabethan part of the college, but it was refaced in 1854 and is not now remarkable. Inside the First Quad, which is small and almost domestic, the eastern half of the south range – on the left on entering – is more evidently Elizabethan; the rest of the quad is Jacobean and very agreeable. The north range, on the right, consists of the chapel, 1636, with its east window on The Turl, and the Principal's Lodging adjoining its west end. The chapel is pleasant but unremarkable; the screen and the pulpit are 17th-century. There is a bust of Lawrence of Arabia who was an undergraduate here and was later a Fellow of All Souls.

In the west range, facing the gatehouse, the hall was built in 1617 and has a contemporary screen; the hammer-beam roof was covered with a ceiling in 1741, with the consequence that its appearance is less interesting than the similar and exactly contemporary hall at Exeter across the street.

Beyond the hall the inner quad is architecturally more homogeneous, despite having been built over a span of seventy years from about 1640 onwards. In the north range (on the right) there is a passage to the Ship Street range, built in 1908 by the college surveyor; and to the west is the Third Quad formed by the Old Members' Building of 1971. The south side of the college buildings is on Market Street, where there are ways into the Covered Market. But first the visitor should see Lincoln College.

Jesus College, First Quad

Lincoln College, Turl Street. Founded 1427 by Richard Fleming, Bishop of Lincoln, as The Rector and Scholars of the College of the Blessed Mary and All Saints, Lincoln, in the University of Oxford.

The college was founded before the Reformation by Bishop Richard Fleming, with the primary object of combating the Lollard 'heresies' by teaching young priests to defend the true theology and the mysteries of Scripture. Fleming obtained Royal consent to his uniting the three parishes of All Saints, St Michael, and St Mildred, and diverting their revenues to his college; in exchange the college was to provide chaplains for the parishes. It still appoints the Vicar of St Michael's.

The church of St Mildred was demolished immediately and college building was begun on the site; but progress was very slow. Fleming died in 1431 without having obtained any further benefactions; and the revenues of the three parishes were inadequate. There were improvements when Thomas Rotherham – Fleming's successor as Bishop of Lincoln – in 1479 gave the college new statutes and further endowments, from which he came to be known as the second founder.

The Reformation frustrated the college's main religious objective, and in Elizabeth's time it was obliged to adhere to the Church of England. Its fortunes improved from the 17th century and there were eminent men among the Fellows, including Dr John Radcliffe; even so, it remained small and far from rich. In the 18th century Lincoln became prominent for having among its Fellows the young John Wesley, who used to hold in his rooms meetings of The Holy Club. In the following century the scholarly Mark Pattinson, who became a Fellow in 1839 and Rector in 1861, did a great deal for Lincoln's standing.

Lincoln College, Front Quad

The Front Quad is small and modest, and is virtually all of the 15th century; opposite the gatehouse is the hall with its original collar beams, wind-braces, and smoke-louvre; the screen is thought to date from 1700, and the Gothic fireplace is known to be of 1891. In the centre of the south range there is a passage leading to the Chapel Quad, completed in 1631. The chapel itself, in the south range, is of this date, and so is the interior woodwork; also contemporary is the remarkable series of stained-glass windows by Bernard van Linge, Abraham's brother.

Around the central buildings that form the two quads several additions have been squeezed into the confined site. The most visible of these is the new Rector's Lodging, 1930, with its front on the street. Other additions include the Grove Building, 1883, and a small library of 1906. Lincoln also owns buildings on the other side of The Turl, including *The Mitre*, which as a hostelry dates from the 14th century, though the present buildings are mainly of the 17th. It was then a famous coaching inn, and more recently a superior family hotel. It is now a link in a chain of restaurants, and the upper rooms have been converted into living quarters for members of Lincoln College.

All Saints Church. The most important – even dramatic – addition to Lincoln's buildings is the former church of All Saints, at one time the City Church. It was built in 1708 on the site of a medieval church, to designs attributed to Dean Henry Aldrich of Christ Church, perhaps assisted by Nicholas Hawksmoor. The church was converted into Lincoln's library by Robert Potter in 1971–5; *Pevsner* describes it as one of the most perfect English churches of its date, with none of the baroque violence of Hawksmoor's churches and yet with more force than Gibbs's.

The Covered Market, 1772. Carfax. This, as its name implies, is a permanent roofed building; it has entrances in The High as well as in Market Street. It is a brightly lit maze of shops and stalls, put up in the first place by the City expressly to clear the congestion of barrows that in the 18th century choked the streets of Carfax. The Market now includes a courtyard, with an entrance in The Cornmarket, once that of the Golden Cross Inn. Adjoining are private offices containing *The Painted Room*, with elaborate 16th-century murals, which may normally be seen on application. In the 16th century this building was part of The Crown Inn belonging to Shakespeare's friend John Davenant; it is believed that Shakespeare stayed at The Crown on his journeys between London and Stratford, and he was certainly godfather to John's son William Davenant, later Poet Laureate.

Across the Cornmarket is *Carfax Tower*, once the belfry of St Martin's Church, where in the medieval riots the bells were rung to summon the citizens. The nave was demolished in 1896 to ease the traffic congestion; the mechanical 'quarter-jacks' on the front of the tower, formerly inside the nave, are replicas of the 17th-century originals.

In 1610 a magnificent conduit or drinking fountain was presented to the City of Oxford by Otho Nicholson, Treasurer to King James I. It was erected at Carfax, and water was piped to it from Hinksey Hill; on festive occasions it ran wine for the citizens. It was eventually found to be an obstruction, and in 1787 it was removed to Nuneham Park, where the landscaping by Lancelot Brown made a good setting for it.

From the Covered Market this itinerary crosses The High and follows St Aldate's southwards. The street is dominated by Tom Tower above the principal gatehouse of Christ Church, which the itinerary will reach later. First, on the left is the Town Hall of 1897 by Henry T. Hare, ponderous and well-suited to its purpose. Across the road the Central Post Office, good Victorian Gothic. On the same (west) side St Aldate's is joined by Pembroke Street, at the other end of which is the excellent *Museum of Modern Art* housed in a converted brewery.

Next after Pembroke Street is St Aldate's Church, of little architectural interest but important as the centre of a large and vigorous evangelical congregation. It is doubtful whether there was ever a saint of this name, which is thought to be a corruption of Eldad or Olave, or simply of 'old gate'.

Pembroke College, St Aldate's. Founded 1624 by Thomas Tesdale and Richard Wightwick, as The Master, Fellows and Scholars of Pembroke College in the University of Oxford.

The college forms two sides of Pembroke Square and has its main gate in the south-west corner. It was founded nominally by James I, but actually by the trustees of two worthies of Abingdon, who wanted to found a college for their own kin and for boys from Abingdon School, and it was named for the Earl of Pembroke who was then Chancellor of the University (his statue is in the Old Schools Quad). The college occupies the site of Broadgates Hall, Beef Hall, and four smaller medieval halls; and along the St Aldate's front the buildings include a row of almshouses begun by Cardinal Wolsey in 1525 but left unfinished; they are now the Master's Lodgings.

Pembroke College, Old Quad

The first quadrangle – the Old Quad – is basically 17th-century, but it was modified, gothicized and raised by another storey in the 1830s. On the right a doorway leads into Chapel Quad, which is all of the 19th century, except for the chapel itself, of 1732, on the left. Externally this is a modest-looking building, but within it is richly ornamented baroque, skilfully restored, and retaining the original stalls and screen; the painting above the altar is a copy from Rubens. On the far side of this quad is the fine hall of 1848.

Pembroke is noted for having put up with the unruly, eccentric, indigent Samuel Johnson for about four terms in 1728–9; he did not graduate but always remembered Oxford appreciatively. Another remarkable, though less celebrated, member of the college was John Lemprière, who compiled his great *Classical Dictionary* in 1788 while he was still an undergraduate. Another, whose name has outlasted many others in the USA was James L. Smithson who died in 1829 leaving a substantial legacy for the founding of the Smithsonian Institute in Washington DC.

The college has been enlarged in recent years by an additional (north) quadrangle contrived out of the former Beef Lane and now consisting of a mixture of 16th and 17th-century domestic buildings and some 20th-century additions. To the south the site is bounded along Brewer Street by a stretch of the old city wall.

On the other side of Brewer Street is Christ Church Cathedral School, founded in 1546 for the education of boy choristers, of whom there are today about forty who sing at Christ Church, and at Exeter and Worcester Colleges.

Campion Hall. Adjoining the school in Brewer Street is *Campion Hall*, a Jesuit theological college founded in 1895 when Roman Catholics were readmitted to the University, and named after Edmund Campion, a Fellow of St John's College, 1557 to 1569, who later went to Ireland and to Douai. He was an active exponent of the Roman faith, and when he returned to Elizabeth's Protestant England he was arrested in 1581 as a political subversive, and martyred in London. Today's *Campion Hall* is the only building in Oxford by Sir Edwin Lutyens, opened in 1936. It has the status of a Permanent Private Hall.

Back to St Aldate's, with a fine view of Tom Tower, but no admittance yet to Christ Church. A right turn down St Aldate's leads to *The Old Palace*; now occupied by the Roman Catholic Chaplaincy of the University.

A few yards farther, at No 83, is the shop that is said to have inspired Lewis Carroll's knitting sheep in *Through the Looking-Glass*.

At this point visitors may either cross St Aldate's and go through the iron gate into Christ Church Memorial Garden, or they may continue down St Aldate's to Folly Bridge. This course leads past the Faculty of Music on the east side, which houses the impressive *Bate Collection* of musical instruments, and, on the west side, the Magistrates' Courts adapted from a former Morris Motors showroom.

Folly Bridge. The structure standing today was built in 1827 to replace the medieval bridge that formed part of the Grandpont causeway. The handsome warehouse converted into a pub and restaurant is of about the same date. The earlier bridge had a gatehouse reputedly used in the 13th century by Roger Bacon as an observatory and laboratory, and known long afterwards as Friar Bacon's Study or Folly. The small building at the beginning of the bridge, now serving as the office of the boat-hire business below, was built in 1844 as a toll-house. Beyond this the eccentric brick-built house with statues in niches dates from 1849 and, though it may be a folly, has nothing to do with Friar Bacon.

College Barges. For a little longer than a century, from the 1840s until the 1950s, the colleges maintained each its own elegant ceremonial barge, moored on the river bank of Christ Church Meadow. The row of barges stretched for perhaps a quarter of a mile downstream from the bridge; they served both as changing rooms for the boat crews and as grandstands for the spectators, notably in Eights Week in the summer term. Some of these elaborately ornamental craft were originally acquired from City of London Livery Companies, who had used them in the ceremonial river processions of earlier reigns; others were commissioned and built locally. Regrettably inadequate attention was paid to preventing the decay of these old barges; one by one they were condemned and removed, and none remains along the Christ Church reach.

From Folly Bridge this itinerary returns up St Aldate's, past the Police Station and the Faculty of Music, into Christ Church Memorial Gardens and the Broad Walk, once an avenue of old elms. To the left there is a pathway leading to the Meadow Buildings of Christ Church, in effect a side-door of The House where the visitor may be asked to pay a toll.

Restored college barge, now on the Thames near Moulsford

Christ Church – The House, St Aldate's. First founded 1525 by Cardinal Thomas Wolsey under the patronage of Henry VIII; refounded 1546 by the King under a governing body shared by the Cathedral and the College: The Dean, Canons, and Students of the House of Christ in Oxford.

Cardinal Wolsey was a Magdalen scholar and a man of vision. In 1525, when he was at the height of his power as King Henry's counsellor, he obtained Papal licence to suppress the Priory of St Frideswide and a score of minor religious houses, and to appropriate their revenues to built and endow a grandiose *Cardinal College* on the site of the Priory. Wolsey conceived for Oxford a huge and magnificent college to house an even more majestic intellectual force; the buildings would have surpassed any in Oxford, and the chapel would have rivalled that of King's College, Cambridge.

However, in 1529, with the great college only half built, Wolsey fell out of favour with Henry VIII and died in the following year. In 1530 the King, true to his avowed respect for learning, appropriated Wolsey's buildings and revenues, and in 1532 set the college on its feet as King Henry VIII College. After the Dissolution of the Monasteries he in 1546 added the neighbouring monastic Canterbury College to the foundation. King Henry's refoundation of Wolsey's college was on lines more modest than the original grand conception, but he was aware of the advance of the 'New Learning' in the Classical Humanities, and his statutes provide for Regius Professors of Hebrew, Greek, Civil Law, and Medicine, as well as the more traditional Divinity. He made the Dean and Chapter of the new Cathedral the governing body of his college, whereby he not only achieved some economy of operation but also created a hybrid institution

Christ Church, The Meadow Building with The Hall

95

embracing the *Cathedral Church of Christ* and the college, renamed the *House of Christ in Oxford* and usually referred to as 'The House'.

The entrance into Christ Church through the Meadow Buildings leads into the oldest remaining parts of St Frideswide's Priory, namely the 12th-century cloister, rebuilt in the 15th century, and the original, virtually untouched, 13th-century Chapter House, which now contains a souvenir shop and a display of the college silver.

From the cloister one route leads into the Cathedral and another to the huge hall built by Wolsey in the 1520s, when it was the largest in England. It is approached up an early 19th-century stone stairway beneath an elegant Gothic Revival fan vault of about 1640. The hall is notable for its massive decorated hammer-beam roof, built it is said with specially selected Irish oak trees. There is an ante-chamber instead of the more usual screen, and a large array of portraits.

A right turn at the foot of the hall stairs leads into the Great Quadrangle, the largest in Oxford, which was only half built when Wolsey died; only the hall, part of the west range, and the gatehouse – without Wren's tower, of course – were in place. The quad was eventually completed, more than a century later, to Wolsey's planned dimensions, and in the same style, but without the arcading that would have made it a cloister. The gatehouse was completed in 1682 by the addition of a bell-tower designed by Wren for Dean John Fell.

The bell 'Great Tom' was brought from Oseney Abbey at the Dissolution and hung in the gate-tower overlooking the Great Quad, soon afterwards known as Tom Tower and Tom Quad. The statutes drawn up by Henry VIII required that a bell be rung at 9 o'clock in the evening to announce the closing of the gates, one stroke for each member of the House. The members then numbered 100, and another was added in 1664. Great Tom tolls 101 strokes at 9.05 p.m., which is 9 o'clock at Oxford's meridian of I°15" West of Greenwich. The other bells brought from Oseney Abbey are hung in the 19th-century tower above the vaulted entrance to the hall; they are named *Hautclere, Douce, Clement, Austin, Marie, Gabriel, and John.*

The well-known fountain in the centre of the Great Quad was installed after the buildings were completed; the figure of Mercury is a 20th-century copy of a Renaissance original by Giovanni da Bologna. In the south-east corner of the quad, close to the entrance to the hall, a double archway leads to the west door of the Cathedral Church.

Christ Church – The Cathedral, St Aldate's. Building of 12th-century on site of 8th-century chapel of St Frideswide.

Structurally today's Cathedral is the former priory church of St Frideswide dating from the mid-12th century. It became the college chapel of Wolsey's Cardinal College, but would have been demolished when a much grander chapel had been built at a later stage. The church became a cathedral after King Henry's creation of the Diocese of Oxford in the Reformation; it continued, nevertheless, to be the college chapel, and still is today.

A survey of the Cathedral's chief architectural features occupies eight pages in *Pevsner* and cannot be emulated here. Most noticeable is the unusual construction of the main arches of the choir and nave, resulting in the much lower arcading of the side-aisles and a general impression of smallness, accentuated by Wolsey's shortening of the original church when he cut fifty feet off the west end to make room for his Great Quad.

Tom Tower and one of the Christ Church custodians

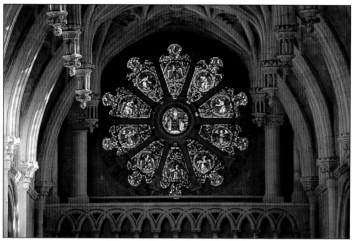

Rose window in the Cathedral

The superb 15th-century Perpendicular vaulting of the choir is thought to be by William Orchard whose work is prominent in the Divinity School. The decorative rose window in the east end and the elaborate reredos below it are the work chiefly of George Gilbert Scott in the restorations of 1870–6.

At the eastern end of the north aisle the Lady Chapel contains the reconstructed shrine of St Frideswide, and beside it a rare watching loft of about 1500 – a wooden cage-like structure from which the shrine could be kept under observation.

In this chapel and elsewhere in the Cathedral there are stained-glass windows by Edward Burne-Jones and William Morris, and by the 17th-century van Linge brothers; there is also some 14th-century glass.

Christ Church Cathedral is widely known for its music; in term-time interested visitors may enquire about choral evensong and other services.

Tom Tower, The Hall, Alden Cottage and Memorial Gardens

Christ Church – The House (continued). Returning to Tom Quad from the Cathedral, a right turn leads along the east range to a narrow vaulted archway, with the 19th-century Fell's Tower above it, which opens out into Killcanon Passage and Peckwater Quad, built in 1705–14 to the design of Dean Henry Aldrich. The fourth side of the quad is occupied by the library, designed by Dr George Clarke, begun in 1717 but not finished until 1772. West of Peckwater is Blue Boar Quad, a modern range fitted into a small space in 1968.

The Hall

On the other side of Peckwater – that is, to the east along the length of the library – is Canterbury Quad, which derives its name from the monastic Canterbury College, absorbed into Christ Church at the Dissolution. On the south side of this quad, to the right after passing the library, is the excellent modern Picture Gallery containing a large collection of Renaissance drawings and paintings.

The grand classical Canterbury Gate into the outer world is by James Wyatt and was built in 1773. To the left out of Canterbury Gate lies Oriel Square with Oriel Street in the far corner and a view of St Mary's spire. Along the east side of the square are the buildings and main gate of Oriel College.

Oriel College, Oriel Square. Founded 1326 by Adam de Brome, Rector of St Mary's, as The Provost and Scholars of the House of the Blessed Mary the Virgin in Oxford.

This foundation is the fifth in seniority. Under the patronage of Edward II de Brome diverted the revenue of St Mary's to his college, which thereafter was responsible for appointing the vicar. De Brome's foundation of 1326 was confirmed by Edward III. The name Oriel is of uncertain origin and has prompted many conjectures. Unlike several other colleges, Oriel has no perceptible regional bias or school connection.

Today's buildings on Oriel Square and those forming the Front Quad are of 1620–40, except that the portico over the door into the hall – with the pierced parapet reading REGNANTE CAROLO, built in the reign of Charles I – was reconstructed in 1897; the statues are taken for Edward II and Charles I with the Virgin Mary above them. The hall, 1637–42, has its original hammer-beam roof, but the screen is 20th-century. The chapel too is of the same period, with contemporary woodwork including a notable communion rail.

The Back Quad, to the north, is a century later than the Front, and its north side is filled with a splendid Palladian library of 1788 by James Wyatt. Beyond the library is St Mary's Quad, parts of which survive from the medieval St Mary's Hall, incorporated into Oriel in 1902. The domestic-looking timber-frame house on the right is not older than 1743. On the far (north) side of this quad is the Cecil Rhodes Building, which faces The High; it was put up in 1908–11 with a large bequest from Cecil Rhodes, who had been an undergraduate at Oriel.

Oriel has always been noted for its intellectual standards, and it was especially prominent in the first half of the 19th century when The Oxford Movement was conceived by a group of the

Oriel College, Oriel Square

college's Fellows including John Keble, John Henry Newman, Thomas Arnold, and Canon Edward Pusey from Christ Church. (*See Keble College*)

A left turn out of the main gate of Oriel, and left again at the corner of the building, leads into Merton Street, where the first gateway on the right is the entrance to Corpus Christi College.

Corpus Christi College, Merton Street. Founded 1571 by Bishop Richard Fox as The President and Scholars of the College of Corpus Christi in the University of Oxford.

'Corpus' was the last college founded in Oxford before the Reformation, by one of the last of the powerful churchmen-statesmen who had virtually ruled England throughout the Middle Ages. Richard Fox was Lord Privy Seal to Henry VII and Henry VIII, and successively Bishop of Exeter, Bath and Wells, Durham, and Winchester; he was Chancellor of Cambridge University and he was a friend both of Erasmus (who was then lecturing at Cambridge) and of Wolsey. Bishop Fox founded Corpus for the

Corpus Christi College with Merton Tower

training of secular clergy in the 'New Learning', the classical humanities; and the college statutes created the University's first formal lectureship in Greek. The Fellows were of course secular clergy and they were forbidden, on pain of expulsion, to join any monastic order, which was the rule also at Merton.

The college stands on the sites of six medieval halls; even so it is small and has only one true quadrangle, the Front Quad, which is the original of 1517 but re-faced in 1937. The pelican at the top of the column-sundial in the quad appears in the coat-of-arms of Bishop Fox, and it symbolizes the Body of Christ, the college being so named. The column was put up in 1581, and the perpetual calendar was added early in the 17th-century. This pelican is not the 16th-century original, which became badly eroded, but a modern replacement carved by the Oxford sculptor Michael Black.

The hall on the east side (left on entering the quad) has its original hammer-beam roof of 1517 and a fine screen and panelling of about 1705. The chapel is reached through a door in the south-east corner; it is of the same date as the rest of the quad and it contains excellent woodwork, screen and stalls, of the late 17th or early 18th century. The altar painting is a copy of Rubens' *Adoration of the Shepherds*. The brass eagle lectern is the only pre-Reformation example in Oxford. Among the muniments saved from destruction in the Civil War is Bishop Fox's crozier, an outstanding piece of Tudor silver-gilt work.

Beyond the chapel, to the south, is the Fellows' Quad; it is not strictly a quadrangle but rather a narrow yard with a cloister-like arcade along one side and the Fellows' Building of 1712, by Dean Henry Aldrich, facing it on the other side. A doorway in the centre of the building leads into the Fellows' Garden, with views across the garden of Christ Church and the Meadow beyond. In the north-west corner is the President's Lodging, partly 17th-century.

Back in the Front Quad, a doorway in the east range leads to the Emily Thomas Quad, where the principal building is the kitchen, said to be part of the 15th-century Urban Hall.

From Corpus it is only about a hundred yards along Merton Street – the only cobbled street remaining in Oxford – to Merton College. The massive tower of Merton Chapel overshadows the street at this point. A footpath to the right, Merton Grove, leads through an iron gate southwards to Merton Fields and Christ Church Meadow, 'One of the most excellent pleasaunces, from which are there obtained beautiful views of the cathedral, of Merton and of Magdalen Tower.' (L. Rice-Oxley, M.A. *Oxford Renowned*)

The pathway running eastwards along the city wall below Merton is Dead Man's Walk. (*See Botanic Garden*) North from Merton Street is Magpie Lane; leading to The High.

Merton College, Merton Street. Founded 1264 by Walter de Merton as The Warden and Scholars of the House or College of Scholars of Merton in the University of Oxford.

Merton is one of the three oldest foundations in Oxford and is the first college to have received formal statutes. Walter de Merton was another powerful churchman-statesman,

Merton College over Merton Field

Lord Chancellor to Henry III and later Bishop of Rochester; his aim was to educate secular priests – with a preference for his own kin – for the administration of Church and State, in opposition to the monastic orders who had dominated and restricted the advance of learning.

Walter de Merton set up his college with preliminary statutes in 1264 and definitive statutes in 1274. The Fellows of the college were of course in secular holy orders and were forbidden, on pain of expulsion, to join any monastic community. The college became noted in the 14th century for its progressive thinking, not without accusations of heresy when John Wycliffe was a member. In later centuries Merton led the advance in astronomy, mathematics and medicine.

Mob Quad Library

Henry Savile appears to have been elected a Fellow in 1565 at the age of fifteen; he was Warden from 1586 until he died in 1622. He founded the Savilian Professorships of Geometry and of Astronomy and made Merton a leader in the academic field, especially in the sciences. One of Savile's notable contemporaries was Thomas Bodley, whose monument is in the chapel.

Before going into the college, it is worth looking at the grotesque heads that adorn the magnificent bell-tower. There is also a beautifully carved tympanum over the principal gate; the gatehouse is of 1418, and the carving is thought to be of about 1420; it shows the Book of the Seven Seals (*Revelation V*) flanked by the Lamb and a Unicorn, with the Lion behind; to the right the kneeling figure of a bishop is taken to be Walter de Merton, accompanied by John the Baptist. All this in a forest of luxuriant trees, with birds, burrowing rabbits and other animals. The statues on the gatehouse, of the founder and of Henry III, are replacements of the originals.

The college buildings span about six centuries from the foundation in the 13th to the additions of the 19th. The main gate leads into an asymmetrical Front Quadrangle, with the hall immediately opposite; this is said to date from the foundation but has twice been so heavily restored that little of the original subsists, except for the authentically 13th-century door with elaborate wrought-iron decoration. The hall is not normally open to visitors, but the door may be seen at any time and is worth a moment's attention.

To the left, in the far, south, corner of the quad, there is an archway of about 1497, its vaulting decorated with finely carved signs of the Zodiac; it leads into the Fellows' Quad of 1608–10, austere but adorned on the south range with a four-tier frontispiece in the style of, and contemporary with, those in the Old Schools Quad and at Wadham College. The sundial in this quad was designed by a Fellow of the college in 1974, to replace one of the 18th-century. Another passage, in the north-east corner of the Front Quad, leads into

Merton College Fellows' Garden

St Alban's (or 'Stubbins') Quad, named after the medieval St Alban's Hall, acquired by Merton in 1549, and rebuilt in 1910 by Basil Champneys.

Back in the Front Quad, the west side is formed by the end of the chapel, with a sundial on one of the buttresses. In the south-west corner of the quad a passage leads under the Muniment Tower into Mob Quad, said to be the oldest complete quadrangle in Oxford, built in stages in 1304–78; it houses in the south and west wings the oldest library in England. Conducted visits to this library may be arranged with the Curator, whose office is in the passage under the Muniment Tower. The Curator may also allow access to the room occupied by Max Beerbohm, now a small museum of his memorabilia.

From Mob Quad a narrow passage leads to the door of the chapel, the oldest and the largest of the college chapels. It was planned as a traditional cruciform design on the scale of a small cathedral, but the nave was never built; thus the choir and the transepts form a T-shape, which was later adopted at New College, Magdalen, All Souls and elsewhere. Building was begun in 1290 and the choir was completed about 1295, but the crossing and transepts were not finished until 130 years later, in 1425, and the bell tower only in 1450. The eight bells are of the late 17th-century.

The chapel has a fine east window containing some original 13th-century glass and valuable 15th-century panels moved from the ante-chapel. The glass in the side windows, cleverly restored in 1931, is also of the 13th century and is an unusually complete and early example of a design that became general in England in the following century. The altar painting is a good Crucifixion of the school of Tintoretto; the brass lectern, facing both ways, is of 1500 and is considered outstandingly fine. The screen between chapel and ante-chapel is a 20th-century modification of work by Wren.

The chapel and Mob Quad stand partly on the site of the medieval parish church of St John the Baptist, which explains the presence of St John in the carving over the main gate; Walter de Merton was allowed to demolish the church only on condition that his chapel should also serve as the parish church, which it did until 1891. This may have influenced his decision to build on so large a scale.

Opposite the main gate of the college, on the other side of Merton Street, is Postmasters' Hall, built in 1290 and rebuilt in 1580; alongside it is the former Warden's Lodgings, in grand 1908 neo-Jacobean style; it now houses the college's law and science libraries.

In the 1370s a Fellow of Merton left a legacy for the support of nine poor scholars, who were to receive a *portion* of the commons given to the Fellows, and were to be called *Portionistae*, which was corrupted to 'Postmasters'. At the beginning they were boys who sang in the choir, waited on the Fellows in the hall, and studied when they could. They were lodged in the building across the street. Today the term 'Postmasters' refers to undergraduate scholars. (*See Demies at Magdalen*). Behind Postmasters' Hall is a 16th-century 'royal' or 'real' tennis court.

The most convenient way to return from Merton to The Broad is along Magpie Lane (opposite The Grove) across the High Street and into Radcliffe Square. From here the itinerary goes down Brasenose Lane, with its medieval kennel, into The Turl, then into The Broad and so to the Martyrs' Memorial. Across St Giles is the entrance to Beaumont Street, which begins, on the left or south side with the yellow brick High Victorian pompus Gothic of the Randolph Hotel, and on the right the imposing neo-Grecian mass of the *Ashmolean Museum.*

Ashmolean Museum, Beaumont Street. This building was opened in 1845 as the University Galleries housing the art components of Elias Ashmole's great collection, with later additions.

The east wing, with its front on St Giles, is not part of the museum but the home of the *Taylor Institution*, the centre of modern language studies containing the modern European languages library. The illogical presence in the same building of these two dissimilar institutions is the consequence of coinciding benefactions; the Revd Francis Randolph and Sir Roger Newdigate towards the end of the 18th century made donations for a new museum building, for which plans were drawn up in the 1830s, simultaneously with a bequest from Sir Robert Taylor to set up an institution to improve English students' knowledge of other European languages.

A little farther down Beaumont Street, on the left (south) side is the *Oxford Playhouse*, a modest and attractive building of 1938 by Sir Edward Maufe. For several reasons the Playhouse has had difficulty in fulfiling a role as the University Theatre, despite the efforts of interested people to make it viable and the enthusiasm with which drama is presented.

A little farther along Beaumont Street the houses on both sides are elegant Georgian buildings providing an agreeable approach to Worcester College, which stands squarely at the far end facing up the street.

The Ashmolean Museum

Worcester College, Worcester Street. Founded 1714 by Sir Thomas Cookes on the site of Gloucester College of 1283 as The Provost, Fellows and Scholars of Worcester College in the University of Oxford.

The college stands on the site of the medieval monastic foundation of Gloucester College, set up in 1283 by the Benedictine monks for their scholars from Gloucester Abbey, and later from other abbeys in the south of England. At Gloucester College each abbey set up its own small house or *camera*, built as part of the group for protection and to share the hall and chapel; by the middle of the 14th century fifteen abbeys were represented.

Gloucester College was dissolved in 1539 along with the monasteries, and in 1560 the buildings were acquired by Sir Thomas White, who had recently founded St John's. It became Gloucester Hall and continued precariously as a subsidiary of St John's for about a century and a half; the buildings were then bought by Sir Thomas Cookes, a rich Worcestershire baronet, and in 1714 it was endowed and refounded as Worcester College, with the last Principal of the old Hall, Richard Blechinden, as first Provost.

Among Blechinden's friends was the amateur architect Dr George Clarke. Under his guidance, possibly with advice from Nicholas Hawksmoor, building work at Worcester began in 1720; it continued until about 1790, but even then the design remained incomplete.

Dr Clarke, besides being the chief architect of the college, was also an important benefactor; during his lifetime he founded fellowships and scholarships, and when he died in 1736 he bequeathed to the college his valuable collection of books, manuscripts, and architectural drawings.

Worcester College Main Gate

The principal gate, with the library above it, is recessed in a forecourt formed by the projecting wings of the hall (left) and the chapel. Both were built to Clarke's plans in the 1720s, designed internally by James Wyatt in the 1780s in the manner of his time, and redesigned in the 1860s by William Burges, in florid Victorian; the hall has since been restored to Wyatt's design, but the chapel remains much as Burges left it. In the chapel is an alabaster lectern in the Italian Renaissance style, of 1865. The library, not normally open to visitors, is reached by a remarkable circular stone staircase which can be seen if not ascended. The central, and only, quad is markedly asymmetrical because the original design was never fully carried out. The gateway gives into an arcade, with the library above it, looking over the sunken lawn. On the left is a row of six medieval cottages (*camerae*), survivors of the fifteen that made up Gloucester College;

Library and Front Quad

they are not old enough to date from the original foundation in 1283, but they are certainly of the 15th century. On the right the north range, on its embankment, is mainly the work of Dr Clarke, though not built until 1759, some years after his death. The building at the western end, the Provost's Lodgings, facing the garden beyond, was designed by Henry Keene some twenty years later.

The fourth side of the quad is a plain wall beyond which, through an archway at the far end of the *camerae*, is the garden – better described perhaps as a park – with its lawns, magnificent trees, and famous lake; and, as a walk round the garden reveals, Worcester has been able to expand in its ample territory without the contortions imposed on colleges with restricted sites. In the south of the grounds are the Nuffield Building, 1939, the New Building, 1961, the Wolfson Building, 1971 and another building completed in 1990. North of the Provost's stable yard is the Besse building, 1954; and in the north part of the grounds, overlooking the lake, is the Sainsbury Building, 1984, by Richard MacCormac.

Visitors who prefer a moderate 'perambulation' may turn right along Worcester Street, past the vulgar new buildings known as Gloucester Green, to the junction with New Road on the left. On this corner stands *Nuffield College*, easily identified by its tower and tall green spire.

Energetic visitors interested in seeing *Jericho* may turn left out of Worcester College into Walton Street. A short way along, by a sunken pathway, is Worcester Place with *Ruskin College* on the corner and in the west wall a gate back into Worcester College.

Ruskin College; It was named after John Ruskin as a social reformer. The primary objective of the college is to provide residential two-year courses, mainly in social studies, for working men and women. Ruskin College is not a constituent of the university but its students can obtain university places and can graduate. The college is financed partly by the Trade Unions and Co-operatives and partly by central government grants; it works in conjunction with the Open University and the Workers' Educational Association.

The Oxford University Press. Farther along Walton Street is the OUP in the classical-fronted building that it has occupied since 1830 when it moved from the Clarendon Building. Behind Daniel Robertson's ponderous front is an attractive grassed quadrangle with a large beech tree; unfortunately it is not ordinarily open to visitors. There are, however, fine modern buildings adjoining the central quad to the west, accessible from Great Clarendon Street.

The OUP began its existence in the 16th century largely for printing and disseminating ancient manuscript texts; in the early 19th century it obtained a Bible-printing privilege from which it made large profits. Later in the century it ventured into publishing, especially scholastic text-books for which there was a great demand. In the 20th century dictionaries and reference

Oxford University Press

books have supplanted Bibles as the principal source of earnings. A notable achievement was the publication in March 1989 of the second edition of the *Oxford English Dictionary* in 20 volumes containing half a million definitions, including words that entered the language as recently as the 1980s.

St Paul's Church. Across Walton Street from the OUP, facing down Great Clarendon Street, is St Paul's, a neo-Grecian church of 1836 by H. J. Underwood. It became redundant in the 1960s and was to have been demolished, but it was rescued by the Oxford Area Arts Council, with the idea that it might become a community theatre for the performing arts.

Jericho. Beginning at Great Clarendon Street, beside the OUP, and stretching north and west for about half a mile, is Oxford's first working people's suburb of the early 19th century. Jericho reflects the arrival of the Oxford Canal in 1790, the Eagle Ironworks in 1825, and the OUP in 1830; it is a fairly large area of modest terrace houses that was spared the fate of other districts such as St Ebbe's – demolished in the 1950s – and has been restored and in places rebuilt without loss of character. The western boundary is the Oxford Canal, where there are two boatyards and a picturesque gathering of canal boats.

St. Barnabas and the Oxford Canal

Beside the yards is *St Barnabas Church*, 1869, built at the personal expense of Thomas Combe, Printer to the University (Head of the OUP). He required the architect, Arthur Blomfield, to put up a well-built church of good proportions, without any costly decoration, for a congregation of a thousand. Blomfield, with a design based on a Venetian basilica, was outstandingly successful and produced a most attractive church. In its early days it was the chief place of worship of the Oxford Movement, of which Combe was a keen supporter.

Jericho is now a valued suburb only a few minutes' walk from the city centre, and, with the decline in manual employment, it is becoming more middle-class in character.

Nuffield College, New Road. Founded 1937 by Viscount Nuffield (W. R. Morris) Opened 1958.

Viscount Nuffield, the motor magnate, offered the University one million pounds to set up a college for social research; though he had little sympathy with the sociologists, he was interested in promoting exchanges between academic and other sorts of people. The college, being wholly devoted to research, admits only graduates and does no teaching; it was one of the first colleges to admit women as well as men.

Lord Nuffield in 1937 bought as a site the terminal basin of the Oxford Canal, which had long ceased to carry any commercial traffic; the start of building was delayed by disagreements over designs, persisting far into 1939 until all building was excluded by the approach of war. Work was eventually begun in 1949, and completed in 1960. Lord Nuffield criticized the

Nuffield College spire with river and canal

University for the slowness of progress – both academically and architecturally – but he was finally satisfied when in 1958 the college ceased to be a dependency of the University and acquired full collegiate status. When he died in 1963 he endowed the college with the remainder of his considerable fortune.

The buildings are arranged to form a double quadrangle on two levels – the lower part has a lily-pond – with more the appearance of a country-house courtyard than of a college quad; the quad alone is open to visitors on weekdays. Nuffield has no formal chapel; the plans included one but its construction was deferred, and later it was found not to be required. A small upstairs room furnished as a chapel is apparently adequate. It has stained glass windows by John Piper and Patrick Reyntiens.

The most imposing, if not entirely congruous, feature of the college is its eleven-storey tower, which houses the library, surmounted by its narrow green spire. It has been much criticized, but it has been part of the Oxford spire-scape for many years and has come to be accepted.

The Mound and other features. Facing Nuffield across New Road is The Mound, or Motte, some 60 feet high. It was part of the castle defences built by Robert d'Oilly from 1071, when it was topped by a timber watch-tower. It is accessible to officially conducted parties but the views from the top are less interesting than those to be had from buildings nearer the centre.

Beyond The Mound is County Hall, a severe Gothic building looking like a prison; and indeed Oxford County Gaol stands behind it. Within the prison precincts is the bell-tower of

St George's chapel, the only survivor of six towers guarding the inner bailey of the Castle.

New Road continues up to Bonn Square, with the County Library and the Westgate Centre on the right; also on the right is a pedestrian road, St Ebbe's, which goes down to the western end of Pembroke Street, to St Ebbe's Church, and to the Museum of Modern Art. Straight ahead from Bonn Square is Queen Street, entirely commercial, ending at Carfax. On the left in the square is the New Road Baptist Church, 1819, and a memorial garden; beyond the garden a pedestrian way leads into New Inn Hall Street – once known, it seems, as the street of the Seven Deadly Sins perhaps after an inn so named – and to St Peter's College.

St Peter's College, New Inn Hall Street. Founded 1929 by Dr Christopher Chavasse on the site of New Inn Hall (1476) as The Master, Fellows and Scholars of the College of St Peter-le-Bailey in the University of Oxford.

St Peter's stands on the site of New Inn Hall, set up in 1476 on the foundations of an even older house known as Trilleck's Inn. During the Civil War, in the 1640s, New Inn Hall was taken over by King Charles to house the Royal Mint, where silver objects given by the colleges were melted down for coinage. It afterwards continued as an academic hall until 1887 when it was acquired by Balliol and used as a residential annexe.

In 1874 the parish church of St Peter-le-Bailey was moved from inside the Castle bailey and rebuilt close to New Inn Hall and near an 18th-century stone-faced building that had been the offices of the Oxford Canal Company. The Rector of the parish, the Revd Henry Linton, bought this building in 1878 to serve as his rectory.

A later Rector, the Revd Francis Chavasse, had the idea of founding a college for 'Low-

St. Peter's College, Linton House

Church' men of modest means, but he died in 1928 before he could achieve his aim. His son and successor as Rector, Dr Christopher Chavasse, with financial help from Lord Nuffield, carried out the idea; in 1929 he bought the Hall – by then consisting of sound 19th-century buildings – added the rectory, and refounded it as St Peter's Hall, alongside his parish church, with himself as the first Master. When the parish of St Peter's was amalgamated with St Ebbe's the church was made redundant and became the chapel of the foundation. In 1961 St Peter's Hall acquired full collegiate status and changed its name accordingly.

About the same time St Peter's bought Canal House in Bulwarks Lane with its heavy pedimented porch, to be seen from New Road, and made it the Master's Lodging, thus leaving Linton House (the old Rectory) free for college use. Standing back from the street with lawns and a large tree before it, it is now the principal entrance. With the help of several benefactors including Lord Nuffield (again) and M. Antonin Besse, the college has expanded into other buildings; the most important of these is the former Central School for Girls, 1901, now cleverly integrated into St Peter's amalgam and appropriately named the Chavasse Building.

The Oxford Canal Company. The southern section of the Oxford Canal, designed to connect the Midlands with Oxford and the upper Thames, reached the city in 1790, terminating in a large basin with wharves and coal-yards, where Nuffield College now stands. In 1797 the Canal Company put up in New Inn Hall Street an office building then named Wyaston House; and in 1829 Canal House was built overlooking the basin to serve as the Manager's house and as offices. Wyaston House was later sold to the Rector of St Peter's parish, the Revd Henry Linton, and later still, in 1929 when St Peter's Hall was founded, it became Linton House; it is now the principal building in the street front of St Peter's College.

On the other side of New Inn Hall Street an ancient archway is the entrance to Frewin Hall, originally St Mary's College, one of the monastic houses, founded in 1435 as an Augustinian priory, but dissolved in 1539. It is now an annexe of Brasenose College; parts of the gateway are original, but the buildings within are 18th and 19th-century, modernized in the 1960s.

A little farther down New Inn Hall Street, on the same side as St Peter's, is the Wesley Memorial Methodist Church of 1878, chiefly remarkable for its high steeple.

To the right, opposite the church, is St Michael's Street leading to the Cornmarket; about half-way along is an entrance to the Oxford Union Society, with its recently restored Pre-Raphaelite wall paintings; it is not normally open to the public.

Oxford Union Society. 'The Union' was founded in 1823 under the name of the Oxford Union Debating Society, and changed to its present title in 1825. It soon became a nursery for budding politicians, would-be parliamentarians, and other users of words, to practise Commons-style debating. The Union has fostered innumerable MPs, several Prime Ministers, including Harold Macmillan (Lord Stockton) and Edward Heath, barristers (Quintin Hogg, Lord Hailsham), with diplomats, civil servants, writers and broadcasters (Sir Robin Day). In keeping with the times, women are playing an increasingly important part in the Union's affairs; the first woman President was elected in 1968, succeeded by others including Benazir Bhutto in 1977.

On the other side of the street is Vanbrugh House, distinguished by its giant pilasters flanking the doorway, said to be a 'minor work' of the architect of Blenheim Palace, but more probably a parody by Vanbrugh's chief stone-mason Bartholomew Peisley who lived here. St Michael's Street ends at the Cornmarket; this wholly commercial street incudes several 16th and 17th-century buildings behind the vulgar shop-fronts, as may be detected here and there. Immediately opposite is Ship Street and the City Church of St Michael-at-the-North-Gate.

St Michael-at-the-North-Gate.

The tower, but not the nave, is the oldest building in the city; it is Saxon, of about the year 1000, certainly pre-Conquest. Adjoining the tower and spanning the Cornmarket was the old Bocardo Prison for debtors and prostitutes, where the three Protestant Bishops were held in 1554–6 before they were mar-

St Michael-at-the-North-Gate

tyred. The North Gate and the prison were demolished in 1771.

The nave and chancel of the church date from the 13th century but they have been rebuilt, damaged by fire, and restored, to such an extend that the architectural details are far from clear. There is a 14th-century font which was at St Martin's, Carfax before that church was demolished. Of great interest are four panels of 13th-century stained glass set in the east lancet windows; this glass is older than the glass at Merton and is possibly the oldest in Oxford. In the north aisle there is an unusual panel of 15th-century glass depicting a Crucifixion on a lily, flanked by Seraphim.

The tower contains, from the ground upwards, a library (used during services as a 'crying room' for infants); a treasury with ancient documents and valuable silver vessels, combined with a museum of interesting objects; a clock mechanism; six bells; and, five storeys up, the roof with views of the city

ITINERARY IV and Outlying Places

This brief 'perambulation', as *Pevsner* would call it, includes some of the less publicized, but nonetheless interesting establishments. From the intersection of streets at the eastern end of The Broad near Blackwell's this itinerary follows Holywell Street as far as the junction with Mansfield Road on the left. A short distance along it is Jowett's Walk on the right and Harris Manchester College on the left.

Harris Manchester College

Harris Manchester College, formerly a Permanent Private Hall, obtained a Charter in 1996, and its full name is now The Manchester Academy and Harris College. Its origin is a Dissenting Academy for Nonconformist ministers' training founded in Manchester in 1786; it moved from Manchester to London in 1853 and to Oxford in 1889, some years after the University Tests Act of 1871 which eliminated religious restrictions and admitted Nonconformists to Oxford. The College has retained 'Academy' in its name to indicate its origins and has now added the name of its benefactor Lord Harris of Peckham, whose financial support has enabled the foundation to become Oxford's thirty-ninth college.

The buildings in Mansfield Road are of 1891–3 and include a Victorian Gothic chapel with a set of windows by Edward Burne-Jones and William Morris; there is also a substantial library.

Mansfield College, Mansfield Road. Founded in Birmingham in the 1830s as a theological college in what is now the United Reformed Church, Mansfield came to Oxford in 1886, some years after the opening of the University to Nonconformists. In the 1950s it became a Permanent Private Hall, and in 1995 a fully federated college.

Today Mansfield's undergraduate membership is not confined to ordinands but includes a majority reading with other aims. The college buildings, at the northern end of Mansfield Road, deserve attention as one of the major works of Basil Champneys, completed in 1889.

Mansfield Road joins South Parks Road in the centre of the Science Area which, as already observed, is more remarkable for the achievements of the scientists working here than for any architectural feature. At the eastern end of South Parks Road stands a large red-brick building known as Cherwell Edge.

Linacre College, St Cross Road. Founded 1962 by the University for graduates from other universities. It was first set up in the Worthington Building in St Aldate's as a non-residential society; it moved in 1977 to the much larger building of Cherwell Edge, where in 1985 it erected a substantial new block, the Abraham Building, in the architectural style of the original house of 1887. It thus became able to meet, with a building of architectural merit, the demand for residential as well as merely dining and common-room provisions.

Opposite: Early winter on the Thames at Port Meadow

St Cross Building. St Cross Road. Where Manor Road meets St Cross Road stands the modern St Cross Building also known as the Law Library; it houses the Bodleian law collection, the English Faculty Library, and the Institute of Economics and Statistics. The building is by Sir Leslie Martin & Colin Wilson, 1964; *Pevsner* is enthusiastic about it, with reason.

St Cross Church. On the other side of the road is St Cross Church; it dates from the 12th century and retains its chancel arch of that period, and a west tower and aisles of the 13th century; the rest, for the most part, including the painting on the roof , is 19th-century. The church serves as the chapel of St Catherine's College. The churchyard contains the graves of many well-known academic and literary people.

Holywell Manor. Next to the church is the 12th-century Manor of Holywell; the house was rebuilt in the 16th century but little of that structure remains. It was occupied over the centuries by many different tenants, including the Clewer Sisterhood, who added some sort of buildings that have disappeared except for a wall with windows between the Manor and the church. The Manor has been in the possession of Balliol since 1930, and is run jointly with St Anne's as a graduate house. Its most attractive feature is the garden.

St Catherine's College. Manor Road. St Catherine's is the larger of the two Oxford colleges wholly designed and built since the Second World War. After the abolition of servitors, St Catherine's Society was set up in 1868 for the matriculation of non-collegiate students of modest means; they were able to read for a degree without the expense of college membership.

St. Catherine's College, Main Quad

St Catherine's had a succession of homes, until an appeal in the late 1950s brought in many handsome donations, from Dr Rudolph Light and others. Buildings were commissioned from the Danish architect Arne Jacobsen, and completed and opened in 1964. *Pevsner* says: 'Here is a perfect piece of architecture'. St Catherine's is also interesting for its cleverly designed garden setting and general air of spaciousness.

St Catherine's Society achieved college status and changed its name accordingly in 1963; since moving into its new buildings it has become numerically one of the largest colleges.

The way back to the starting point is along St Cross Road and *Holywell Street*, which is not only an elegant sequence of 17th and 18th-century houses but also pleasant to walk in, being closed to traffic.

Templeton College, Kennington. Set up in 1965 as The Oxford Centre for Management Studies, with a gift from Clifford Barclay to buy the site and put up the first buildings. A major benefaction by Sir John Templeton (a former Rhodes Scholar) in 1983 financed a second building programme and a parallel expansion of didactic activity, which led to the Centre's becoming in 1995 the thirty-seventh federated Oxford college and changing its name accordingly.

Templeton College

Oseney and Osney. The Abbey Church of Oseney stood where there is now a cemetery beside the railway line as it enters Oxford from the South; the other monastic buildings of Oseney stretched as far as the bank of the Thames. The church was huge; it had the third tallest spire in England and many richly decorated altars. Oxford was one of the new dioceses created in the Reformation, and at first the Abbey Church of Oseney was designated the Cathedral. A few years later, however, in 1546, the priory church of St Frideswide became the Cathedral and Oseney was abandoned. The former Abbot of Oseney, Robert King, was the first Bishop of Oxford.

The 12th-century village of Oseney was on the east bank of the Thames and shared with the Abbey the area now covered by the 19th-century warehouses, the railway, and the cemetery. Osney Town was laid out and built on the west bank in the 1850s and consists of a compact group of terrace houses arranged in three parallel streets. There is a riverside footpath to Osney Lock and, farther on, to Folly Bridge.

Rewley Abbey was on the branch of the Thames known as the Castle Mill Stream, near today's railway station; it too had an impressive Abbey church, though it never equalled Oseney.

St Thomas the Martyr, Becket Street. There is nothing left of the 12th-century village of Oseney that once clustered round the Abbey, except the church of St Thomas; it is a rather gloomy neglected-looking building in a depressed part of the city, beside the railway, but even so it has atmosphere. It began as a chapel built about 1140 by Oseney Abbey, but only the chancel is of that date; the tower is 'Perpendicular', meaning probably 15th or early 16th-century. Robert Burton of Christ Church, author of *The Anatomy of Melancholy* was Vicar 1616–40.

Outlying Places

Several suburbs or absorbed villages include notable buildings or have been the scene of interesting events. A few such places particularly deserving visitors' attention are mentioned below.

Iffley. The best approach is from Folly Bridge by the towpath that borders the stretch of the Thames (or Isis) where the spring Torpids and the Summer Eights are rowed. The village of Iffley is on the other side of the river, which may be crossed by the lock gates and a footbridge over the weir; its outstanding building is the 12th-century Norman church of St Mary the Virgin. *Pevsner* says: 'A magnificent little church, lavishly decorated with sculpture ... one of the best preserved 12th-century village churches in England', and devotes three pages to describing it. It is, moreover, in a delightful setting.

Iffley lock on the River Thames

Cumnor. The village is under siege from all sides, but manages to retain some identity, at least in the popular old pub, 'The Bear and Ragged Staff', and the 12th-century church of St Michael, which contains some admirable woodwork including medieval pews, a fine Jacobean pulpit, and a rare spiral staircase of 1685 up to the bell-chamber, where there is a fine peal of eight bells, recently restored and re-hung.

It was at the now vanished Cumnor Place that in 1560 Amy Robsart died so mysteriously – found dead at the foot of the stairs. She was the wife of Queen Elizabeth's 'favourite', Robert Dudley, Earl of Leicester, and it was generally believed that she had been murdered. (The story appears in Scott's *Kenilworth*). She is buried in the University Church of St Mary's.

Cumnor church

Wytham. Wytham is a pretty, tidy, village best approached on foot from Godstow, though for motorists there is access from the ring-road. There is an ancient pub, 'The White Hart', with a pleasant courtyard garden and an enormous dovecote in what is now the car park. The church of All Saints is hidden behind the walls that surround the manor house grounds; originally 12th-century, it was rebuilt early in the 19th century and is not remarkable except for some ancient stained glass. The manor house – named Wytham Abbey, though there was never an abbey here – is privately occupied. The wooded hill to the west of the village, Wytham Woods, belongs to the University and is extensively used for nature research. It is open only to permit-holders.

Old Marston. The parish church of St Nicholas dates from 1122, though the oldest parts of the building – the arcading – are Early English (13th-century) with 15th-century reconstruction and a 15th-century tower; an attractive building in a virtually unspoilt village setting. A side road leads to the riverside pub, 'The Victoria Arms', which can also be approached by punt on the Cherwell.

Old Headington. St Andrew's, the parish church, is a Norman building with a chancel arch of about 1160, though the chancel itself is later, rebuilt late 14th century; the site was occupied in Saxon times by a small timber chapel.

Roman occupation of the district of Headington and Shotover left some pottery and bricks, and in Saxon times there was a house or lodge used by the Mercian nobility. It is possible that St Frideswide was a member of one of these families.

Today the old village holds its own against the advancing development on all sides, especially on the side of the John Radcliffe Hospital, which occupies one of the most commanding sites in Oxfordshire. Headington can be reached on foot but it is not the most interesting walk.

Shotover Hill. Shotover Park, covering the greater part of the hill, is the modern survival of an ancient royal forest and hunt; little true forest now remains but there is ample heath and grassland for recreation, and from the high ground excellent views towards the Wittenham Clumps and the Berkshire Downs. On the east side Shotover slopes steeply down into Wheatley.

It was in Shotover, according to a popular legend, that a scholar from Queen's College defended himself from a wild boar by thrusting his volume of Aristotle down its throat, saying 'Graecum est'.

Godstow. The village of Godstow is now an extension of the North Oxford suburb of Wolvercote. It is best approached from the Thames and is about a mile and a half upstream from Medley. A path on the west bank of the river leads to Godstow Lock and to the ruins of Godstow Nunnery, where King Henry II first saw Rosamund the Fair. Over the bridge is the well-known 'Trout' Inn with its terrace overlooking the weir, The inn buildings, it seems, were originally the guest-house of the Nunnery.[2]

Medley and Port Meadow. Medley is a point on the Thames where there was formerly a weir; the weir-keeper's cottage still stands. On the west bank is Bossom's Boatyard and on the east Medley Boat Station; there is an arched iron footbridge over the river, leading to Binsey.

Medley is at the southern end of Port Meadow, said to be England's oldest and largest continuous meadow; it is recorded in the Domesday Book of 1086, and it covers some 400 acres (160 hectares), or more if the nominally separate but contiguous Wolvercote Common in the north is included. Port Meadow is owned by the freemen of the City of Oxford and is used exclusively for animal grazing and human recreation.

Binsey. Binsey is no more than a hamlet but it includes a popular pub, 'The Perch', with a large garden. Also, about half a mile along the lane northwards beyond Binsey, the church and Holy Well of St Margaret associated with St Frideswide, are hidden at the end of an avenue of ancient horse-chestnut trees.[1]

Admirers of the poet Gerard Manley Hopkins should enjoy reading his *Binsey Poplars* after visiting this stretch of the river; the poplars standing now are the second generation, planted soon after the poem was written; they too may have to be felled.

The Vicar of Binsey about 1125–30 was Nicholas Breakspear, the only Englishman to be elected Pope, as Adrian IV.

Port Meadow, Godstow Lock and The Trout Inn

NOTES

1. **St Frideswide.** According to legend Frideswide was the devout daughter of King Didan the Saxon ruler of Oxnaforda around AD 700; she was or intended to become a nun, and she chastely repulsed the amorous advances of King Algar, or Aelfgar, of Leicester. He was not easily dissuaded, however, and he prepared to take the town, and Frideswide, by force. Just in time an angel warned Frideswide of Algar's plan and told her how to escape in a boat that was waiting for her on the river. With two friends or sister nuns she found the boat, 'manned by a youth with a beautiful countenance, clothed in white,' who rowed them away, most probably to Binsey.

Meanwhile Algar, not knowing of Frideswide's flight, attacked the town, but in the act he was struck blind by a flash of lightning, and he abandoned the assault. News of Algar's plight reached Frideswide at Binsey; she forgivingly prayed for him to St Margaret, who appeared in a vision and told her to strike the ground with her staff at a certain spot. When Frideswide did this a spring gushed forth; this holy water, when applied to the now penitent Algar's eyes, restored his sight. Chastened and grateful, Algar decently abandoned his earlier intentions and returned to his estates in Leicester. Frideswide afterwards built beside the well a chapel or oratory, which she dedicated to St Margaret.

King Didan built for Frideswide a nunnery on the site where the Cathedral now stands, where she was Prioress until she died about 740. She was later canonized and adopted as the patron saint of Oxford. She is represented by one of the three crowned demi-virgins on the coat of arms of the Diocese of Oxford.

Binsey. The miraculous properties of the holy water in St Margaret's Well made Binsey a place of pilgrimage, and it was larger in medieval times than it is now. In the 12th-century the primitive chapel built by Frideswide was replaced by a small church which, virtually unaltered, still stands with the Well a few feet from its western end. The Well later became overgrown and was almost forgotten until in 1875 the Vicar, the Revd Thomas Prout, had it cleaned up, with a stone well-head built round it, as may be seen today.

The stretch of the river above Medley, skirting Binsey, was one of Lewis Carroll's favourite boating reaches where, it is said, he entertained Dean Liddell's daughters with his tales. St Margaret's Well is convincingly identified as the inspiration for the Treacle Well in the Dormouse's story at the Mad Hatter's tea party; Lewis Carroll makes a play with the original, now obsolete, meaning of *treacle* – that is, medicinal or healing.

2. **Henry II and Rosamund.** King Henry II (reigned 1154–89) spent much of his time at Beaumont Palace (where his son Richard Coeur de Lion was born) and at the royal hunting lodge in Woodstock.

In the 12th-century there was at Godstow Nunnery a community of Benedictine sisters educating the daughters of the nobility. Here the King saw Rosamund Clifford, aged 15, the daughter of Walter, Lord Clifford, who was a benefactor of the Nunnery. Henry took Rosamund off to Woodstock where he set her up in a house or bower near the royal hunting lodge, 'a house of wonderful working, so that no man or woman might come to her. This house was named Labyrinthus, and was wrought like unto a knot in a garden called a maze'. Only the King, of course, knew the way in. The popular story goes on to relate that Queen Eleanor, being suspicious, found her way into the house with the help of a silken thread – which perhaps she had attached to the King's spur – and there found Rosamund, 'and so dealt with her that she lived not long after'. Historians regard this latter part of the tale as invention, and believe it more likely that Rosamund returned to Godstow, where she later died and was buried in the chapel in 1176, her tomb being inscribed:

hic jacet in tumba Rosa mundi, non Rosa munda;
Non redolet, sed olet, quae redolere solet.

This couplet has been neatly translated:

Here Rose the graced not Rose the chaste reposes;
The smell that rises is no smell of roses.

3. **Town and Gown.** All members of the University, down to the youngest students in their 'teens', were in the early stages of holy orders and wore a long gown that clearly distinguished them from the people of the town. The disproportion between the two communities was apparent as early as 1192, when it was remarked that the clerks (scholars and Masters) were so numerous that the town could hardly feed them; 'they turned a borough into the semblance of a lodging house'. The clerks or scholars were further distinguished from the townspeople by the tonsure, which in theory protected them from personal attack by laymen because any violation incurred the grave displeasure of the Church. In practice the tonsure seems to have added to the bitterness of the strife. During the 13th and 14th centuries there was constant tension and intermittent rioting and fighting between Town and Gown. In 1209 a townswoman was killed by a student; the citizens in reprisal arrested several students and, with King John's approval, hanged them. The scholars were alarmed and left Oxford; many went to Cambridge, where they founded or enlarged the nucleus of another university, and did not return for five years. Further outbreaks of violence were recorded in the 13th century, and there were doubtless others to account for the movements of scholars, for instance to Northampton. In 1334 there was a riot and a large exodus of scholars to Stamford, Lincolnshire, where the University might have remained if the King had not commanded them back to Oxford. From then on, candidates for a Master's degree had to swear never to attend or give a lecture in Stamford – a requirement that was not dropped until 1827. The antagonism culminated in the riots of Scholastica's Day, 10th February, 1354 which went on for several days and resulted in much bloodshed and destruction. The King and the Bishop afterwards imposed humiliating penalties on the burgesses and heaped privileges on the University, giving the Chancellor legal jurisdiction over the lives and affairs of the citizens, down to details such as rents and prices, which had given rise to so many quarrels.

4. **Thomas Huxley and the Bishop.** Charles Darwin's *The Origin of Species*, published towards the end of 1859, had stirred up a vigorous controversy between the 'creationists', who adhered to the biblical explanation of the world, and the 'evolutionists', who found the theories of Darwin and Wallace more credible. The British Association meeting at the University Museum in June 1860, chaired by Professor Charles Daubeny, was very well attended. The principal speaker for the creationists was Samuel ('Soapy Sam') Wilberforce, Bishop of Oxford, seemingly a rather unctuous prelate; the evolutionists were led by the eminent scientist and brilliant speaker Thomas Huxley; the hypochondriac Darwin was not well enough to attend.

The Bishop, after a display of supercilious rhetoric, turned to Huxley and asked him whether it was through his grandfather or his grandmother that he claimed descent from a monkey. Huxley, after a brilliant and scientifically cogent exposition of his arguments, replied to the Bishop's frivolous taunt by saying (his precise words were never recorded) that if he had to choose for an ancestor between a poor ape and a man highly endowed by nature and of great influence, who used his gifts to introduce ridicule into a serious scientific discussion and to discredit humble seekers of the truth, he would unhesitatingly affirm his preference for the ape. It was reported that in the ensuing commotion one lady fainted; as Huxley himself afterwards said, his retort caused inextinguishable laughter among the audience who listened to the rest of his argument with close attention. The Bishop, it seems, knew when he was beaten and made no reply.

Concise Index

Principal entries in bold

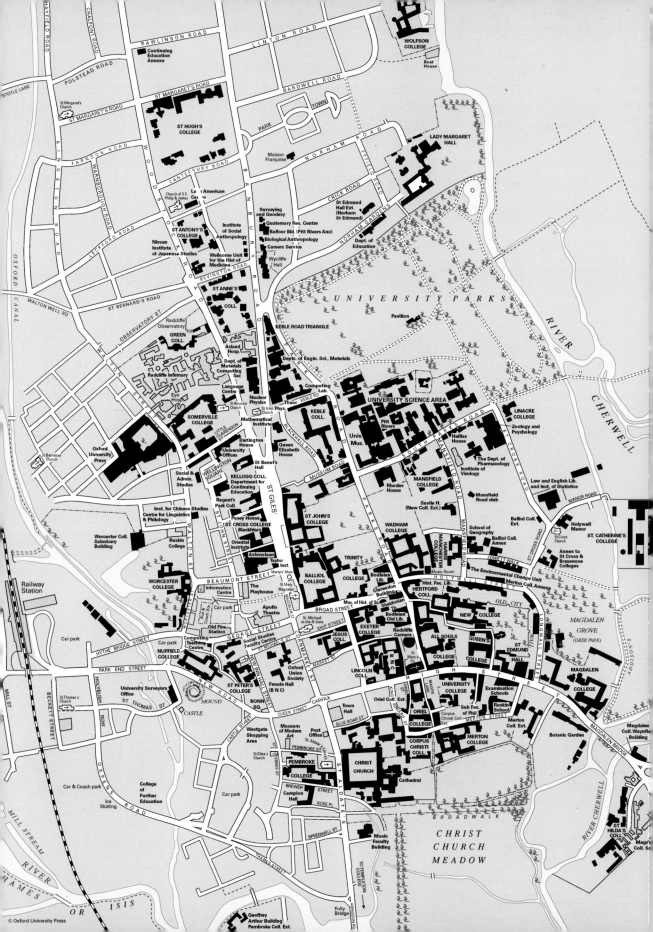